SŌKA GAKKAI

創価学会

SŌKA GAKKAI
JAPAN'S MILITANT BUDDHISTS

by Noah S. Brannen
with photographs by Hideo Fujimori

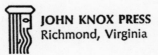

JOHN KNOX PRESS
Richmond, Virginia

TO ANN

whose sensitivity and perception
were companion and guide
on this pilgrimage to encounter

CONTENTS

FOREWORD

A hero of one of Dostoevsky's novels is made to say, "Man has done nothing but invent God so as to go on living and not kill himself; that's the whole of universal history up till now."

In the Battle for Okinawa, the greatest battle of the Pacific War, when the Japanese 32nd Army had been routed out of the mesh of coral caves all up and down the island and finally pushed to the last point overlooking the ocean, with no navy to come to the rescue and no place left to go, General Ushijima arose in the early morning before dawn and, with his officers and men, climbed to the highest point of the peak overlooking the ocean. And here, in the traditional manner of a brave Japanese warrior, the general cut his stomach open. Thousands of his men followed, those without weapons leaping off the cliff to dash their heads on the coral rocks below. Here were men left with nothing to believe in. Unconquerable Japan had met defeat.

Search for a faith to live by would seem to explain the phenomenal popularity of what are called "new religions" in Japan today. When the national faith—faith in the divine origin of the emperor and the divine mission of his subjects—was shattered because of her defeat by the allied powers in the Second World War, Japan was left in a spiritual vacuum with nothing left to live by.

But a vacuum cannot continue indefinitely in either the physical or the spiritual world. Something will rush in to fill the void. The requirement to believe in something in order to live becomes the rationale for believing in *anything*. And this is the condition in which millions of Japanese find themselves today.

This book is an attempt to describe in some detail the case of Sōka Gakkai, the answer of sixteen million Japanese (and some non-Japanese) to the quest for a faith by which a man can live.

The author would like to express his appreciation to the following friends, colleagues, scholars, and acquaintances who have helped in the preparation of this book: to Dr. Joseph Yamagiwa of the University of Michigan, who read the preliminary paper which forms the background of this study and offered many helpful suggestions; to William P. Woodard, former editor of *Contemporary Religions in Japan,* and Director of Research for the International Institute for the Study of Religions, who encouraged the writing of this book and published several preliminary articles on this subject by the author; to members of the staff of the International Institute, especially Yoshirō Tamura, who made valuable corrections of the original manuscript; to Professor Keiji Nishitani, formerly of the Department of Philosophy of Kyōto University, who spent many hours reading and correcting the manuscript and offered valuable suggestions from the point of view of a Buddhist scholar; to numerous acquaintances among the believers in the Nichiren Shō faith who patiently answered innumerable questions from the author, and among them especially to Priest Jigaku Mizutani, the General Director of Taisekiji; Shirotaka Watanabe, head of the Student Department of Sōka Gakkai at that time and now representative to the National Diet; and Kazuya Morita, Assistant Executive Secretary of Sōka Gakkai; to William Elliott, missionary colleague, who carefully read and corrected the manuscript and made invaluable suggestions concerning the literary style; to Dr. Paul S. Minear and Dr. Richard Gard, both of Yale University, who carefully read the manuscript and offered criticism and encouragement; and finally to Michiko Ōtake (formerly Miss Asō), personal secretary and research assistant, without whose help this study could not have been accomplished.

In addition I am grateful for the opportunities given me to lecture on numerous occasions over a period of three years to groups of missionaries and national Christian leaders in Japan on the subject of this study. An unusual opportunity was afforded me to visit Okinawa for a period of ten days during the spring of 1963 to give lectures and take part in discussions in Japanese with Okinawan Christian leaders. While in Okinawa, I was able to meet with chaplains and American military personnel to discuss the significance of the spread of Sōka Gakkai among American servicemen, to appear in an interview on television, and to speak in Japanese on a radio broadcast.

N.S.B.

International Christian University
Mitaka, Japan
July, 1968

Iwashi no atama mo,
shinjin kara

Worship of the head of a sardine,
this too is faith

(A Japanese proverb)

一章 THE "THIRD WORLD POWER"?

Tomoji murdered his son. On a Saturday afternoon, March 6, 1965, he took a baseball bat and crushed the skull of his son, just returned from Tokyo. A neighbor from a nearby farm found Tomoji in a back room of his farmhouse, staring at the lifeless body of the twenty-seven-year-old young man lying on the dirt floor. But the heart of the village went out to Tomoji. The heart of conservative, rural Japan was with the old father who had murdered his eldest son—his heir. The son, caught up in the frenzied, fanatic fervor of Sōka Gakkai, had returned to the old homestead to demolish the Buddhist and Shintō god-shelves and convert his father to his new-found faith. "I warned him not to destroy the god-shelves. I warned him!" cried the old farmer, driven almost insane by the realization of what he had done. "I warned him, but he wouldn't listen. Why wouldn't he listen to me? Why?"

It is time that someone took in hand the task of answering the question of old Tomoji and the questions of many like him both in Japan and in America and throughout the world who have become alarmed at the growing power of Sōka Gakkai, the religious sect which not only threatens to take over Japan but also claims for itself a mission to save the world.

By and large the majority of the Japanese people have been introduced to Sōka Gakkai through the same channel which has brought the name into the limelight in America in recent years— through the secular press. Interestingly enough, one American claims to have been converted to Sōka Gakkai because of reading an article in LOOK. He is a professional violinist. Another American, a Texan, says that he was so struck by the unfair bias of an article which appeared in the *Herald Examiner* that he began an investigation to disprove what the reporter had written and was eventually converted. Since it is the sensational which makes news, Sōka Gakkai is known chiefly for its political success, underhanded activities in campaigning, techniques of pressure and intimidation in matters of religious faith, involvement in legal suits over burial rights, and iconoclastic fanaticism. For the average Japanese his introduction to Sōka Gakkai has not been a casual one, to say the least.

Americans and other foreigners living in Japan have had a somewhat more than casual encounter with this religious faith. Some American servicemen (most of them married to Japanese) have become converts. In most cases a Japanese girl friend or wife plays an important part in the conversion. As the Negro serviceman who operates the movie theatre at Tachikawa Air Base explained it, "I was converted because I noticed what a wonderful change came over my wife when she joined."

"What attracted you to Sōka Gakkai?" the author asked Boatswain's Mate First Class, Harold Grant. "For the first time I found true religion," he answered in a matter-of-fact tone. He had attended a Baptist Sunday school as a boy because his mother had insisted upon it, but when he entered the Navy he drifted away. Religion to Americans, he feels, has meaning only on Sunday; it has no relevance to daily life. "True religion," to this sailor, is religion which constitutes a vital part of man's total life, and something which he can have in his own home (without "going out on Sunday to get it"). Religion, if it is true, he said, includes the whole man—the whole family. Religion, he believes, if it is real, makes a difference in the believer; his life should show a definite change, and he should experience immediate material benefits which he can personally enjoy in this life.

Among the "benefits" which the Grants feel this faith has given them was the wife's miraculous cure of migraine headaches which had been accompanied by occasional blackouts. She had been going to a doctor at the naval base for over a year but did not feel that he was sympathetic to her complaints. Usually he would tell her to take an aspirin and go to bed. After joining Sōka Gakkai, however, when she went to the base to see the doctor, she was examined by a new doctor who treated her and she was completely cured.

The author (left) is standing at the entrance to the Taisekiji Temple with a friend who is a member of Sōka Gakkai.

Sōka Gakkai members arrive by the busload to visit Taisekiji Temple.

Photographs by Hideo Fujimori,
staff photographer for *Bungei Shunju*.
(Used by permission of *Bungei Shunju*.)

Members of the women's division of Sōka Gakkai arrive at Taisekiji Temple.

The two leaders of Sōka Gakkai, President Daisaku Ikeda and Abbot
Nittatsu Shōnin.

Abbot Nittatsu Shōnin leads a procession.

The tomb of Jōsei Toda, postwar leader of Sōka Gakkai, is located at Taisekiji Temple.

A large lecture hall provides modern facilities at Taisekiji Temple.

President Ikeda goes to the front of the platform and leads a pep song.

Taisekiji's Grand Reception Hall and snowcapped Mt. Fuji.

The temple's facilities include a recreation building.

Americans also are attracted to Sōka Gakkai.

The Japanese are converting to Sōka Gakkai by the thousands. In 1963 the president of Sōka Gakkai reported that they were winning 20,000 new converts a month. One Christian missionary remarked, in a voice of consternation, obviously having struggled for some time with the question of the reason for the spectacular success of Sōka Gakkai in winning converts, that he wondered if these people weren't of some different race from the Japanese with whom he had been dealing. "In converting people to their faith they do everything we were told not to do. What we were told simply would not work in evangelism in Japan they have worked to advantage. The techniques they use to win millions we were told would turn the Japanese away. What is the secret?"

So far as the techniques of mass psychology employed by Sōka Gakkai leaders in their rallies and jamborees are concerned —military-like reviews with troops of young men and young women, fife and drum corps, "folk-music" festivals, political campaigning, pilgrimages to the head temple—there is nothing new here that American Christian revivalism hasn't known and employed for over a century.

But one is tempted to answer "yes" to the bewildered missionary; there is a sense in which the millions of converts to Sōka Gakkai are a new race, sought out and "reclaimed," and re-established as "true Japanese" and desirable citizens by the personal evangelism of Sōka Gakkai lay converts. Coal miners who for generations had been faced with one of two alternatives —tight, impersonal labor unions or starvation—now have the option of a third alternative, Sōka Gakkai. For the struggling lower classes who had not counted for much in a highly stratified traditional society Sōka Gakkai offers a chance to come up in the world. The small merchant in a store-front house, the fish dealer who could not afford a market on the main street, the chrome plater who sets up his vats in the back alley, all have found support and mutual benefit opportunities in Sōka Gakkai.

Sōka Gakkai "reclaimed" a ponpon girl (prostitute) married to an American G.I. When her family and friends and society disowned her, Sōka Gakkai welcomed her and gave her a place. Not only were they interested in her, they saw in her a potential missionary to foreign lands. Reclaimed, too, was the washwoman who had never had any of the opportunities of the postwar generation for education, travel, or leisure. Sōka Gakkai introduced her to a world she had never known or expected to know, educated her (in the doctrines of the sect, of course), and put her in touch with other washwomen who had been reclaimed.

To be sure Sōka Gakkai has converts among the intellectuals and the upper classes as well. The priests of the sect are the respected priests of the Buddhist denomination from which Sōka Gakkai springs (the Nichiren Shō Denomination). The leaders of Sōka Gakkai (laymen) would no doubt have climbed to positions of leadership in the secular world. Sōka Gakkai politicians were not all nurtured in the faith, but some established politicians have been "reclaimed" for the religious purposes of Sōka Gakkai. Youth, who believe that tomorrow belongs to them, are attracted by Sōka Gakkai's active, progressive program and its ironbound organization and discipline which seem to offer solidarity in a rather unstable postwar society.

For approximately fifteen percent of the Japanese population the face of Sōka Gakkai has been neither political nor organizational nor controversial, but rather the affable one of a "savior" appearing at the right moment in the midst of personal and national spiritual despair. Sōka Gakkai, to the believer, is a religion, the true religious faith which alone saves man in these last days when the Buddhist Dharma (law, truth, faith) has become decadent and ineffectual.

Sōka Gakkai, on the Japan scene today, is a name that signifies the spiritual mobilization of a great segment of the population. It is no doubt the spiritual strength of Sōka Gakkai to which the youth leader (later to become the present president of the organization) referred when he announced in a rally in 1957 that Sōka Gakkai is to be the "Oriental Third World Power."

> For the reconstruction of Japan in her current perilous situation, wedged in between the battle encampments of the East and West, we youth must grasp firmly the life philosophy of The Holy One, Nichiren, which provides us a faith guide

far excelling Soviet Communism or America's Pursuit of Wealth ideas, and, with this Oriental Third World Power as our base, make this mission of the Japanese people known to the world.

Whatever this leader meant when he used the term "Third World Power," the phrase has an ominous ring when one recalls the "New Order in East Asia" or "The East Asiatic Co-Prosperity Sphere" of prewar days in Japan. Could Sōka Gakkai be a resurgence of rightists pledged to push Japan to the world military front? Many have looked at the military-like organization of this group and concluded that it is definitely aimed at organizing the Japanese people into a religious army to compete with the two great military blocs of the world. The leadership of men like Hōjō (charter member of the Board of Directors of Sōka Gakkai and National Diet member), who was trained in Japan's number one military academy, only adds to the anxiety concerning the ultimate purpose of the organization.

"Third World Power" is now a watchword of Sōka Gakkai. Seizing upon this phrase in the youth leader's speech the organization has exploited it for propaganda purposes. "The Third Civilization" is the title of one of the periodicals of the sect. The members believe themselves to be part of something new, something really big. This belief is verified in their own eyes by the phenomenal growth of the organization from 3,000 members when it was resurrected after the war, to over sixteen million in 1967.

This "watchword" got a restatement after the House of Councilors' election in July, 1962, when Sōka Gakkai emerged as the "Third Force" in the Upper House of the National Diet. What indeed is the direction in which this organization is moving? What does this spectacular success in winning converts and placing political candidates mean from the point of view of established religious groups and political parties in Japan? What significance does this have in Japan's relations with other nations? Is Sōka Gakkai in fact the idealogical base for a new internationally powerful Japan, as the Shintō religion was used in the period leading up to World War II? An introduction to this religious faith certainly seems to be in order.

* * *

The setting for our first meeting with a devout believer was our own living room, Japanese style, on a small island in the Japan Inland Sea. A friend whom we had known since we first arrived in Japan in 1951 had come to welcome us back from a brief furlough in the United States. Or so we thought. We greeted her at the door, invited her in, served her coffee and cake, as we had always done. But she was obviously embarrassed. "I'm ashamed to be treated like a guest," she began. We soon learned why; she had come to convert us. She had come to win Christian missionaries to her newly discovered faith.

Soon she produced her literature and began her propaganda. Sōka Gakkai is her whole life now. "I have fifty souls in my hand," she began. This was an ordinary housewife, without any special talent or education. She goes at her own expense to the head temple at the foot of Mt. Fuji three times a year. She reads the literature prepared (in ever increasing quantity) by the organization, and takes examinations given at certain intervals. She spends a large part of her husband's salary every month on Sōka Gakkai expenses. Needless to add, she has converted the husband.

"What do you mean when you say that you have fifty souls in your hand?" I asked. "Why, they depend on me. I am their leader in the faith. Not only do we meet to study the teachings in my home, but I have to keep in touch with them to see if they are sick, or in trouble, or in need of help in any way." She has had a telephone installed in her home at a cost three times her husband's monthly salary so that she can keep in touch with the members in her charge.

Here was a transformed woman. Even the look in her eyes was so strange it made us wonder if this indeed were the woman whom we had known before.

This woman was one of the first people we had met in the neighborhood where we lived in a small Japanese tea-house before we were able to build a home of our own on the island. She was young, with no children, and her husband worked until late every night. She seemed to be in need of a friend. We heard one day that she had had a miscarriage, and so my wife called on her. Little by little a friendship grew up between our two families. We soon discovered that she had never been able to have children. This seemed to be the source of an incessant loneliness and discouragement. Evidently it was also leading to estrangement between herself and her husband.

The wife had time on her hands. First she studied cloth dyeing; then it was German. We encouraged both the husband and wife to learn English from us at home on our free evenings, and this seemed to bring the two of them together for a time. On his day off the husband came over to put in some extra wall plugs for us. In this period they both began to take an interest in singing and joined a choral group together. The husband was influential in getting a group of men employees in his shop to help with a Christmas concert given by our church choir. Now and then we talked about Christianity and our own faith. They seemed to be interested in this too (for the wife Christianity was, perhaps, another subject to study for a while), but the husband frankly admitted that he felt no need of any kind of religion. As he explained it, he was perfectly healthy, able to work, and, in short, in no particular need of religion.

With this background of association before we went to America on furlough it was quite a shock to meet this changed woman out on her mission to convert us to her faith. The husband, too, had changed. I met him from time to time on the ferry and we exchanged friendly greetings. When I mentioned that it would be nice to have him come over again for a long chat, he replied: "If I were to come, there is only one thing we could talk about." "What is that?" I asked. "It's something you said to me one time. You said that if Jesus Christ had not died on the cross man would never have known what God is really like." "Yes, I said that, I guess; I believe it." "I can't accept a man like him who died a miserable death on a cross," he retorted. "Nor can I accept your kind of God."

For the first time, after a long period of association with this man—of concern for him and his wife—I was brought face to face with the realization of how little he knew of "my kind of God." Now I knew that the husband, like the wife, was bound to use any opportunity to spread his new faith.

"Your faith has no place for God," I answered. "Your faith is what we call humanism. To you man is capable of saving himself by his own effort. You have no object of worship greater than man."

This answer touched on a fundamental difference between his faith and mine—a fundamental difference between Buddhism and Christianity—which I was not aware of at that time, nor did I know how completely mistaken my idea of his faith must have sounded to him. But, because he was hurrying to work, the conversation stopped with this rather dogmatic pronouncement on my part and a look of incomprehension on his face. After this he didn't call on us, either to try to convert us or for any other reason. I might add that our chorus was short on male voices in the Christmas concert that year.

I met the wife again on the train for Tokyo, and, by some odd coincidence, we met the following day on the same train making the return trip. "We have a strong related destiny," she said, interpreting our chance meeting in terms of a Buddhist fatalistic concept. "Surely, there is some significance to our meeting like this."

She had heard that my wife was expecting our fourth child, and she knew of the negative Rh-factor difficulty which we had always had. "You had better give in and believe," she said. "For if you don't, something dreadful is bound to happen to this baby." The doctor had already predicted a fifty-fifty chance for the survival of the baby, and had made preparation for immediate blood transfusions. But a perfectly normal baby boy was born shortly after that meeting on the train, with negative blood like his mother's so that there were no complications at all. I was tempted to write to this friend and tell her that her curse had worked in reverse, but somehow it didn't seem that this would be playing the game fairly.

Not long afterward I received a book through the mail. It was a book in English published by Sōka Gakkai called *The Sōkagakkai*. We didn't have to read the return address on the envelope to know who had sent the gift. The conversation had been taken up again.

Ashiki o harōte tasuke-tamae
Tenri-Ō-no-Mikoto

Sweep away all iniquity and save us,
O God of Heavenly Wisdom

(Overture of the *Mikagura Uta* of Tenri-kyō)

二章 RELIGIONS OF THE HERE AND NOW

As I was walking through an island of the Inland Sea one of my shoelaces broke. In the village there was a cobbler whose establishment—serving both as business and home—was squeezed into a six-foot front on the crowded market street. I stepped into the entrance and saw a busy cobbler squatting on the straw mat (which would no doubt serve as bed when night came). I asked for a pair of shoelaces, intending to take them along and replace the broken one myself. But the cobbler insisted that I take off my shoes, slide into the wooden clogs he had ready for such occasions, and let him replace the strings himself. His face was beaming. Seldom have I seen a face so expressive of the joy of living. It was not long before I discovered the source of his exuberance; it was his religious faith which had become a hidden spring welling up within him until it was ready to burst through at any provocation. He couldn't wait to share it with me. To him I was neither stranger nor foreigner, but another dry, parched soul crying for the waters which he possessed, or which possessed him. An hour and a half later I left the shop with shoes well laced and tied, and a never-to-be-forgotten impression of the sincerity of a simple island cobbler and his faith.

Certainly one constant factor of meaning in the term "new religions" which is commonly used to designate the postwar phenomenon of rising religious sects, is the new factor of personal commitment. The common denominator which unites the postwar sects in Japan is this element of individual or personal faith.

Despite its self-claim to an orthodox tradition of 700 years, Sōka Gakkai cannot be properly evaluated apart from a consideration of other postwar popular religions in Japan. New religious organizations have capitalized on the present situation of spiritual unrest in much the same way that Communism has exploited modern social instability for the spread of its doctrine.

Oguchi, Associate Professor at Tokyo University, finds the root cause for the popularity of the "new religions" in Japan today in the psychological condition produced by the postwar religious vacuum:

> In a word the growth of Sōka Gakkai is because its thought and activities have compatibility with the Japanese spiritual climate. The slogan adopted by Sōka Gakkai, "Make the people happy," is certainly not new with Sōka Gakkai. Sekai Meshi-yakyō, for example, ties social evils to the base of "sickness, poverty, and war" and promises to banish these evils from the world. . . . This kind of religion will flourish as long as the conditions among the people continue as they are.[1]

Of one thing we can be certain, Sōka Gakkai and others among the new religious sects are taking full note of the "conditions . . . as they are," and they are aggressively presenting a program of thought and action designed to fill the current religious vacuum.

Is Sōka Gakkai a "New Religion"?

The fact that Sōka Gakkai was first registered as a juridical foundation in 1952 places it in a similar category with other organizations classified under the term "new religions" (*shinkō shūkyō*). From the point of view of Sōka Gakkai members, however, their organization cannot be classified among the "new religions," and consequently Sōka Gakkai is not affiliated with the national interdenominational organizations—the Union of New Religious Organizations of Japan and the Japan Free-Religions Association. But so far as the Ministry of Education, established religions, and the general public are concerned, Sōka Gakkai is one of a kind with the flourishing new sects.

However, the branding of Sōka Gakkai as a "new religion" has more substantial grounds than its recent registration with the Tokyo municipal government or the mere ill will of rival sects. It has seen the same phenomenal growth that others of the new religious organizations have enjoyed.[2] Further, in an effort to win converts rapidly, Sōka Gakkai has made its own bed among these new sects and has taken on common characteristics of these bed-mates to such an extent that despite its own claim to "orthodoxy" the people in general and the religious world have quite understandably listened to the actions which speak louder than words. While denouncing other new religions as fraudulent and superficial, Sōka Gakkai has offered point by point the same popular attractions which account in large measure for the great influx of members into these sects since the end of the Second World War.[3]

What Is the Definition of "New Religion"?

The next question to settle is the meaning of the term *shinkō shūkyō*. The term may be translated as "newly arisen religious faiths," or "new flourishing religions," but this is not sufficient to clear up the meaning of this term which is ambiguous even among religious scholars in Japan.[4] Some scholars give the term a temporal reference in Japanese religious history, defining it as including those religions which have originated since the beginning of the twentieth century. One authority who defines the term by historical reference is Reihō Masunaga of Komazawa University. He includes only those religions which originated shortly before, during, or after the Second World War. It is quite common, however, to include Tenrikyō (founded in 1838) and Konkōkyō (founded in 1859) among the so-called "new religions."[5]

It is obvious, therefore, that the disparity in opinions among scholars as to which are to be included under the term is due more to a false criterion of classification than to a difference in opinion regarding the similarity of the religions in question. I suggest that the temporal reference is not as important as the possession of common characteristics in determining which religious groups fall into the classification of *shinkō shūkyō*. This is, in fact, what has happened in the everyday use of the term in Japan. To call a religion a *shinkō shūkyō* today is equivalent to labeling it as a fraudulent or bogus religion (*inchiki shūkyō*). The two terms are interchangeable in nonprofessional parlance.

Instead of the term "new religions," the term "unorthodox" would be a handy translation of *shinkō shūkyō* if it were possible to determine what orthodoxy is in Japanese religion. And there are many groups in Japan which hide unorthodox practices behind traditional orthodox names, as, for example, the Sōka Gakkai (which claims to be the "orthodox" branch of Nichiren Buddhism), or the Tenshō Kōtai Jingūkyō (the so-called "Dancing Religion" whose name borrows the characters for the Sun Goddess, Amaterasu, and characters for "Shrine of the Imperial Prince").

"Popular religions" is perhaps the best term to incorporate the various groups which have come to be identified as *shinkō shūkyō*. Or if the translation "religion" is objected to on the basis that these popular manifestations of religious faith are merely splinters from traditional religions such as Shintō and Buddhism, perhaps the term "popular religious sects" would be more appropriate. The term "popular" is more apropos than "new" because it is less specific in terms of time reference, and the emphasis is properly placed upon the appeal of the faith to the masses, which is the chief characteristic which all of these groups have in common.

A rather cursory examination of the "doctrine" and practice of the numerous popular religions gives the following list of characteristics as a standard for classification.

CHARACTERISTICS OF POPULAR RELIGIONS

1. The religion centers in belief in a living person or persons, or the living memory of a person recently dead.
2. The religion contains shamanistic elements (i.e., resort to magic and use of the shaman, who is believed to have special power over good and evil spiritual forces).
3. The religion promises material benefits, now.
4. The religion is aimed at filling the sociopsychological need for "belonging."
5. The religion offers a channel of release for youthful vigor.
6. The religion relieves the individual of the necessity of personal moral decision, and brings consolation that the believer is religious without demanding radical inner change.

7. The religion consciously encourages a sense of continuity with familial and national heritage.

The characteristics listed above are in themselves a summary explanation of the popularity and phenomenal growth of the sects in recent years. Other elements which fall more under the category of techniques, as distinct from characteristics, will appear as we deal more at length with the factors contributing to the success of popular religions.

In the established religions, such as Buddhism and Christianity, none of the above-listed characteristics can be considered to be essential to or descriptive of the faith. It may be contended that some of these elements are to be found in the established religions, however. For instance, Islam has nationalistic traits, and Christianity has a long history of aggressive youth activity. It is true, too, that when established religions become "popularized" they take on other of the above listed characteristics, such as shamanism, promise of material benefit, and so forth. But insofar as a religion is "established" its basic elements are to be found elsewhere than in these seven characteristics.

Shintō, native religion of the Japanese, contains many of the characteristics of popular religions. Notable are its preservation of shamanistic practices, which are basic to many of its rituals, and its conscious emphasis on familial ties and national heritage. Shintō answers the communal instinct through veneration of clan deities and promotion of local festivals. It provides a formal religious outlet without demanding spiritual change or growth within the individual. The great difference, however, between Shintō and the popular religions of Japan today is in the centrality of a contemporary leader as the embodiment of the faith for popular religions. Almost without exception the popular sects have this point in common—their impetus is derived from the spirit of a living leader, or a leader who has only recently died.

A comparison of Sōka Gakkai and other popular religions on the basis of our proposed seven-point list of characteristics will reveal the closeness of that organization to the popular religions, in spite of its claim to "orthodoxy" on the basis of the adoption of traditional Buddhist doctrines.

1. **The religion centers in belief in a living person or persons, or the living memory of a person recently dead.**

Baiyū Watanabe observes that nearly 34 percent of the popular religions of Japan originated with a special revelation which was made to the founder.[6] The people are attracted to this person because they want to believe that what he claims to be true really is true: i.e., that the mysteries of the spiritual world have been revealed in a concrete way to man. This answers what William James calls man's longing for a "new sphere of power."

> When the outward battle is lost, and the outer world disowns him, it redeems and vivifies an interior world which otherwise would be an empty waste.[7]

Case after case could be cited to show how the majority of Japan's popular religions have arisen through faith in the special spiritual revelation and power possessed by the founder. The experience of Nao Deguchi (1837–1918), founder of Ōmoto-kyō (or Ōmoto, as members of the sect prefer to call it), is an outstanding example:

> On January 10, 1892 (according to the lunar calendar) she suddenly entered into a possessed state. Even her relatives thought that she had gone mad. She herself was very much worried whether she had been possessed by an evil spirit or not. . . . As a woman of obedience and diligence she feared if she, possessed by an evil spirit, might seduce the public through the same evil spirit. She wanted to know by whom she had been caught. She visited priests who cast out evil spirits or magicians in order to be examined. It was written . . . that once she had a dialogue with the God who had revealed Himself to her. "She asked, 'What in the world are you?' Then he answered, 'I am Ushitora no Konjin (the God in the Northeast). . . . I am neither a fox nor a badger who usually enter into men. I am the God who re-creates and re-constructs the greater world. . . .'"
> Having received this revelation from the "God in the Northeast," she came to the decision that she would be completely obedient to this God's commands.[8]

The largest popular sects, Tenrikyō, Konkōkyō, Tenshō Kōtai Jingūkyō, Sekai Kyūseikyō, and Seichō no Ie all have

their origin in a special revelation given to the founder. And such revelations are claimed by the founder of Sekai Shindōkyō, Mrs. Hide Aita; the founder of Taidōkyō, Mrs. Shige Nakamura; the founder of Hinomoto Shinseikyō, Mrs. Tsue Okamoto; the founder of Seishōdō Kyōdan, Mrs. Yae Sada.[9]
The content of these revelations seems to be of only secondary importance to the followers. As is true in the case of the founder of Ōmoto, the founder of Tenrikyō was practically illiterate, yet her writings (called *ofudesaki*), though almost illegible, are held sacred by her disciples.

It is in the personality of the leader that the secret of success of the popular religions lies. The real appeal lies in the magnetic power of the venerated founder, whether he be the placid, gentle intercessor who sits at the altar sixteen hours a day to hear the prayers of the devout and relay them to the Great Illuminator (as in Konkōkyō), or the rustic, dynamic teacher to whom members bow for the answer to the most minute problems of everyday life (as in Risshō Kōseikai).

In the writings of Max Weber, the adjective "charismatic" got a new introduction and definition as a description of the type of leadership traditionally given and expected by the Far Eastern peoples. "Charisma" (the noun counterpart of "charismatic") he defines as a quality of authority which a particular person possesses in himself, for which he may or may not make claims; yet whether he does so or not, other men recognize and follow his leadership.[10] It does not seem out of place to relate this "ideal type" to the phenomenon of the strength of these founders of the popular religious sects in Japan. The Japanese are accustomed to bowing before authority.[11] The war tore many props from under the Japanese social superstructure, and one of these primary props was absolute deference to and reliance upon authority. For those who have not found themselves psychologically or emotionally able to make the quick transfer to democracy and its insistence upon the equal status of all men, the charismatic leader—especially in religion—offers a nostalgic tie with the security of prewar days.[12]

Sōka Gakkai's second president, Jōsei Toda, gave the charismatic leadership which the hour demanded, and the masses were

attracted to him. When he interpreted the *Lotus Sūtra* and the
venerated writings of Nichiren, or answered personal problems
from the lectern, he spoke with the unequivocal voice of authority:

> Man's life is eternal. However, I believe no one can precisely explain to you the fact that life is eternal.
> Christianity teaches regarding eternity that a soul ascends to heaven after death and continues to live, but nothing in the world is so ridiculous as this tale. Our lives will exist as they are in perpetuity and we are destined to be born again as a human being. You may be opposed to this statement of mine, saying that it is a mere superstition or that such an idea is ridiculous. But you cannot deny it, for it is true that our lives do exist permanently. You must believe that they really exist eternally. I am the only person in Japan that makes this assertion.[13]

To have been able to sit in on one of Toda's lecture meetings would no doubt have been a rare experience. He usually
finished these meetings with a question and answer period in
which questions were received from the audience. Fortunately
several of these meetings were recorded on long-playing records,
and from these we are able to catch something of the nature of
Toda's personality and persuasiveness.

Toward some of the questioners he was sympathetic and
gentle. A woman had lost her little girl through death and asked
if there were any hope that she might have the child back again.
In answering her Toda spoke to this woman, in a crowd of
over 5,000 people, as if the two of them had been alone together
in his study. He showed a deep, personal interest and sympathy.
In his answer he revealed that he, too, had grappled with the
problem of death. He, too, had lost a little daughter. He told
the woman how he had cried all night holding the dead child
in his arms. And day after day, walking up the hill to his office,
he struggled with the problem of death. What if his wife were
to die! And finally, what if Toda himself were to die! In the
end he had found the answer. It was just because he had found
the answer to death that he had been made president of Sōka
Gakkai, he claimed. His words of consolation to the bereaved

mother were these: I found my daughter again. Whether or not you will discover your dead child again depends upon your faith.

When the occasion called for it, Toda was authoritative in matters of faith. His answer to the question of a young man who was about to return to his home in the country to take over the farm is an example of the positive leadership he gave. The man was worried about his responsibilities as head of the family, which belonged to the Pure Land denomination of Buddhism. He sought Toda's advice. Toda answered that for him, a member of Sōka Gakkai, to inherit his farm where the traditional faith was in Amida Buddha, was no less than the Great Reformation. He said that there should be no question but that the young man should continue in his newfound faith, even if it meant being killed or disinherited. He advised that while the young man was still in Tokyo he should make every effort to strengthen his faith, and that he should not worry about what the morrow would bring. "I could promise you that when I earn yen 100,000,000,000 I would be glad to make you out a check for a million any time you asked. But if you were to try to borrow yen 10,000 from me today I would be a little put out," Toda told him, emphasizing that the young man should set himself to the task of strengthening his own faith today and let tomorrow take care of the needs of itself.

To others he was abrupt and almost brutal. You can't win your husband because you have no faith yourself. You can't win your wife because you're not a good husband. Bring home the bacon and she will listen to your preaching. To a wife who had won her husband but now was upset because he was out until late every night trying to win converts: "You're a fool," the teacher told her before an auditorium full of people. "Your husband's tired of you. He's out playing around and pulling the wool over your eyes. Instead of complaining to him for neglecting you, make him want to stay home. Fix him a hot dinner and keep it ready for him until he gets home. Sit beside him and pour his wine. Stop your nagging and give him something to come home to."

To one woman who complained that she couldn't win others,

Toda said, "You mustn't try to win others! You shall not try
to win others!" To a man who wondered if he should seek to
convert customers who came into his store, the teacher barked,
"You're a fool! Use your common sense, if you have any. The
customer comes to buy your wares; he's not interested in your
religion. Do your evangelizing in your free time, or you'll wake
up one day with your business on the rocks."

He laughed at them and made fun of them. Sometimes he
laughed or cried with them. He tried to make them come back
to their senses if they were too high up in the clouds with their
religion. But when they tried to dig in too deep, as one man
did who asked about the concept of "void," he soon put them
in their places by advising them that they were too ignorant to
understand complicated Buddhist thought.

The fact that Toda had spent two years in prison during
the war because of his religious conviction, together with his
claim to have received the mantle from Makiguchi, founder of
Sōka Gakkai, who was exalted to the status of martyr because
he had died in prison from malnutrition, gave to this charismatic
leader an aura of dynamic magnetism.

So great was the personal power of Toda over the members
of the society that it was predicted that the organization would
fall apart upon his death.[14] The fact that Sōka Gakkai increased
from 800,000 family units to over six million family units in the
ten years after his death is further testimony to the power of a
personality that was able to exert its influence this long after
death.

2. The religion contains shamanistic elements.

In addition to the more sophisticated magical attributes at-
tached to the repetition or intonation of the incantation, *Namu
Myōhōrengekyō* ("Hail to the Wonderful Law of the *Lotus
Sūtra*"), and to the power to heal and bless inherent in the Worship Object (a plaque on which the incantation is written) of
such groups as Sōka Gakkai and Risshō Kōseikai,[15] there are
grosser forms of primitive shamanism which seem to play an
important role in several of the popular religions in Japan today.

The founder of Sekai Kyūseikyō, Mokichi Okada (1882-1955), is said to have possessed a pearl two inches in diameter which he carried in his abdomen from which the healing power of the bodhisattva Kannon radiated. Believers say that it is a ball of light which was bestowed upon the founder from the ball of Kannon's staff. Light is constantly emitted from the spiritual body of Okada, and the believer is able to "tune in" on the light beam by means of charms or amulets. The shaman in Sekai Kyūseikyō treats the sick in a ritual known as *Jōrei*. The recipient kneels before the shaman. The shaman then raises his hand and holds it with the palm turned toward the recipient about eight or ten inches from the ailing part. When the complaint cannot be isolated in one particular area of the body the entire body is made the object of treatment, beginning with the face, then the chest, and the stomach. The recipient then turns around and receives similar treatment directed toward his head, neck, back, and hips. The ritual requires about fifteen minutes. Okada in his later years had sold paper reproductions of the Chinese character meaning "light," written with his own hand. In lieu of the *Jōrei* ritual, when a shaman is not available, this writing can be placed on the sick part of the body to effect the cure.

Sōka Gakkai, along with other popular sects, also promises physical healing, protection from accidents, or personal fortune. These rewards for belief are part of the "benefit" value which, according to the founder Makiguchi, man has in his power to create, but the emphasis in Sōka Gakkai shifted more and more in the direction of reliance upon the magical power of the Worship Object.

The water of the well at Taisekiji, the head temple of Sōka Gakkai, is purported to possess magic healing powers when taken internally or applied externally, and thousands of pilgrims each week receive vials filled with this water to take home with them. It is also believed that flesh is growing on a tooth left by Nichiren (d. A.D. 1282) and enshrined at the head temple. When this tooth was revealed on the rare occasion of the installation of a new abbot (in 1959) the growing flesh was said to have completed the circumference and thus ushered in the time of the "dissemination of the doctrine." The paper Worship Object which each believer places in his home altar has power to bless or curse depending upon one's treatment of it. The simple act of bowing before this Worship Object while intoning the incantation is sufficient to bring the desired result of healing, or business success, or whatever the believer may desire.

Testimonials to the efficacy of the magic of the Worship Object are given by two young people who took leading roles in Sōka Gakkai's Olympics, staged in conjunction with the Tokyo Olympic Games in 1964:

> "Tears for joy ran down my cheeks when I put up the 'Lion Flag,' the emblem of the Sōka Gakkai Youth Division." Tanetada Hino, 18, was proud. Being one of the most enthusiastic believers in the Great Holy One, Nichiren, he was chosen for the honorable job. When it was time for the finale, the 100,000 spectators watched members of the gymnastic team carry an iron tower to the center of the arena. When a human pyramid was completed surrounded by circles of athletes, this young man climbed atop the pyramid and hoisted the flag. From the spectators came a deafening applause. It was a moment of jubilation and excitement—a never-to-be-forgotten moment for the boy, Hino. Having been weak in health and poor, he had made strenuous efforts, intoning the incantation, to achieve the day's success.
>
> Miss Motoko Sato cried for joy while dancing together with other fellow members in the presence of President Daisaku Ikeda and High Priest Nittatsu at the Culture Festival (Sōka Gakkai Olympics). She could not subdue her overwhelming delight remembering the hard days of the past few months. "Suffering from asthma, it seemed impossible for me to take part in the Festival as a dancing member. To make matters worse I almost died from a severe fit about three weeks before that day. However, when I came to myself I was determined to go on to dance at the Festival even at the cost of my life. Then I intoned the incantation, *Namu Myōhōrengekyō*, furiously asking the Worship Object for power to fulfill my desire. The big day came. And I made it! I have never been so grateful to the Worship Object for the great divine benefits."[16]

A man in his sixties brought X-ray pictures to a meeting of Sōka Gakkai in a home in an underprivileged section of Kobe to prove to the author that the incantation had cured him of stomach ulcer. The unfortunate man died within the year of stomach cancer.

Toda claimed to possess the powers of a shaman and laid his hands on invalids to restore their health; these powers were given to him, he claimed, because he had solved the mystery of death. Priests, and some devout followers, claim to be able to make a corpse "soft and light like cotton," through the magic of the incantation. This deliberate defiance of the natural physical process of rigor mortis is proof to the believer that the lost one has been spared rebirth into a lower state of existence.

Takaya Kudō, a priest of this faith, made the following statement to the editors of *Contemporary Religions in Japan:*

> The Great Saint Nichiren on many occasions mentioned the beneficial effects of chanting the *Namu Myōhō-renge-kyō.* Any faithful follower of his teaching, who chants this sacred formula sincerely at the time of death, will show signs of having been saved. For instance, if such a person has a very dark skin and a bad complexion, his skin will become white and beautiful. The weight of his body will become very light like cotton. The substance of his body will become very soft. But those who believe in evil religions will show an opposite condition. . . . This is a phenomenon which medical science cannot satisfactorily explain. . . . When a person dies very peacefully and has an expression similar to that of a Buddhist statue, this shows that during his lifetime he must have held the true faith. I have seen hundreds of dead persons and there has not been a single exception to this rule. The greater my experience has been, the deeper my respect for the words of the Great Saint Nichiren has become.[17]

Interestingly enough, American converts testify to this same phenomenon at the death of a believer. In the interview with Boatswain's Mate Grant (referred to in the first chapter) the author asked concerning Grant's attitude toward this unnatural transformation of the corpse. Grant gave two instances in which this occurred among servicemen. The first instance was the still-birth of a friend's baby in San Diego. The wife had asked her husband to make the incantation three times while she was in delivery, but instead he had gone out to celebrate. The infant was born dead and turned black. Then, incredulous, the father went home in despair. His buddies (also members of Sōka Gakkai) came to his home and began to chant the prayer, *Namu Myōhōrengekyō*. Finally the man joined in, and not fifteen minutes later, it was reported, the dead infant's body began to turn pink, the flesh softened, and the face took on a slight smile. Grant had not seen any of this, but it was reported to him and he believed it.

Another similar incident occurred when a serviceman in America died. He had never been a believer, but his wife (a Japanese) had given him the prayer beads and a "prayer book" of the Sōka Gakkai faith. When he was in the hospital, just before he died, he asked that these things be sent to him and he repeated the incantation while in the hospital. After he died, his body retained its lifelike color, was soft to the touch, and his face had an expression like a Buddhist statue. On seeing this the wife was consoled, for this was conclusive proof to her that he had died a believer. Grant had not seen any of this, but he believed it as it was reported to him.

3. The religion promises material benefits, now.

This characteristic is held in common by all popular religions, and next to the dynamic attraction of the leader to his disciples, promise of material benefits has perhaps the strongest appeal to the masses. It is not difficult to sell a man something he wants. That is just what popular religions are designed to do. It remains for Christianity to awaken a man to the longings that he doesn't know he has; or for Buddhism to teach man to destroy desire.

Not a few of the popular religions make inroads where there is a superstitious fear or dread of the supernatural. Rudolf Otto in *The Idea of the Holy* has defined man's dread of the unknown as the universal basis of religion—the *mysterium tremendum*. All peoples seem to possess a sense of mystery and awe toward higher or unknown powers which determine man's destiny. Japan's native Shintō certainly has evolved from a primitive animism which consisted of a deep reverence for the forces and objects of nature and for spirits of all kinds. In Japan, most people, regardless of their religious affiliation, traditionally have been spiritual sons of Shintō. This is why in a national census many people check both Shintō and Buddhism as the religion of their family. It should not be surprising to find that the underlying "world view" of popular faiths (regardless of the sect) in Japan today is the traditional world view of Shintō.

The Shintō concept of kami ("spirits," or "gods") defines the traditional Japanese "Idea of the Holy." The classic definition of kami is given by the best Shintō scholar and philologist, Motoori Norinaga (1730-1801):

> ". . . it may be said that *kami* signifies, in the first place, the deities of heaven and earth that appear in the ancient records and also the spirits of the shrines where they are worshipped.
> "It is hardly necessary to say that it includes human beings. It also includes such objects as birds, beasts, trees, plants, seas, mountains and so forth. In ancient usage, anything whatsoever which was outside the ordinary, which possessed superior power or which was awe-inspiring was called *kami*. Eminence here does not refer merely to the superiority of nobility, goodness or meritorious deeds. Evil and mysterious things, if they are extraordinary and dreadful, are called *kami*. . . .
> "Furthermore, among things which are not human, the thunder is always called 'sounding-*kami*.' Such things as dragons, the echo, and foxes, inasmuch as they are conspicuous, wonderful and awe-inspiring, are also *kami*. . . .
> "[in the ancient literature] there are . . . instances in which rocks, stumps of trees and leaves of plants spoke audibly. They were all *kami*. There are again numerous places in which seas and mountains are called *kami*. . . . This is because they were exceedingly awe-inspiring."[18]

Kami is a concept which distinguishes between the "profane" and the "sacred." It refers to a holy world of special objects, special personages, and special events believed, because of experience and observation and superstition, to be infused with a greater charge of divinity.

Because of the pervasiveness of Shintō ideology in Japan, even religions imported from abroad have made curious accommodations to this world view which has become so basic a part of the culture and thought of the Japanese people. This explains the phenomenon of a unique "Japanese Buddhism" which is positive and world-affirming, rather than world-negating. It explains, too, the emphasis on material benefits made by the popular religions; for the Japanese (and native Shintō) are basically optimistic, world-affirming, and secular.

The relationship of the world of man and the world of the kami is clearly explained by Dr. Sokyo Ōno, Professor of Koku-gakuin University and a leading Shintō scholar today:

> . . . The world of the kami does not transcend that of man, and man does not need to seek to enter a divine, transcendental world to attain salvation. He seeks salvation by bringing the kami into the human world, into the daily life of the home, the market place, and the cooperation of the people. Man experiences the kami in this world and salvation is attained in the harmonious development of the world. This is epitomized in the myths in which the kami descend from the sacred heavenly country (Takama-ga-hara) to the world of man, which is also the abode of the kami. In worship (*matsuri*), the spirits (*reikon*), the kami, and ancestral spirits are invited to the shrine or to some purified place from the High Heavenly Plain, the Eternal Country; and the evil spirits (*magatsuhi*) are expelled, because they interfere with man's relations with an approach to the kami and ancestral spirits. Therefore, before worship is possible there must be purification. The rite of purification drives away evil, the intruder. But purification does not relieve a person of responsibility for his past acts. On the contrary, it lays this upon him anew. By restoring the original nature of man, one will restore this capacity to do good. At the same time he will become sensible of the obligation to expiate evil and will become able to make amends for his past sins and failures.[19]

The influence of this basic attitude of world-affirmation on Sōka Gakkai is apparent in Toda's teaching concerning the meaning of attaining buddhahood (*jōbutsu*):

> As the Great Holy One, Nichiren, has said, through the merit of the Worship Object, inheriting the karma of the three buddhas, a believer must achieve happiness and comfort before he dies. Even though a man be a thief, if he only believes in

the Worship Object, for some years before death he will be healthy, he'll have money, he'll have peace in his home. How would you like that? You wouldn't complain, would you? . . . That's how it [Nichiren's writing] says it's going to be. If that doesn't happen [to a man in his lifetime] then there's no evidence that he will become buddha after death. Can a man put up with poverty and sickness in this life?[20]

Man's misfortunes, failures in business, unhappiness in his home life, following the traditional interpretation of man's relationship to kami, are the result of irregularity of the four elements of earth, water, fire, and wind; or following the popular (not primitive) Buddhist concept, these misfortunes befall man because of his evil karma. The only hope for man's salvation is for him to enter the new popular religion and trust in the magic of the Worship Object, the incantation, the intercession of the ancestor *kami,* and so forth, to come to his defense.

Faith Healing. Reference has already been made to belief in the power of a shaman to effect the cure of a physical disease. On the part of the recipient, the emphasis is upon the power of one's faith to bring about the cure.

The origin of sickness is variously explained by the different popular religions. Tenrikyō and Seichō no Ie explain that sickness has no place in the eternal destiny of man, and therefore is not real. This explanation follows the same pseudoscientific trend of thought of Mary Baker Eddy (whose writings have been vigorously appropriated by Seichō no Ie). Taniguchi (1894–   ), the founder of Seichō no Ie, denies the existence of sickness and death thus:

> One day when I was in meditation, suddenly I heard an unseen voice, "On earth there exist no sins, no sickness, no death, no poverty! Nothing in the world restrains human beings. Thou art the son of God by nature! Thou art Buddha thyself!"[21]

Miki Nakayama (1798-1887), founder of Tenrikyō, wrote in the Doro-umi Koki that she had received a direct revelation that the soul of man is part of the omnipresent spirit of God, and that the root of suffering and sickness is in the mind. If man sweeps his mind of the eight kinds of "dust" (in Japanese the word for "dust" and the word for "pride" are homophonous) —desire (covetousness), stinginess, misdirected love, hatred (including jealousy and envy), revenge, anger, pride (arrogance), and selfishness (the root of all the others)—and devotes himself to selfless labor for others he will realize the goal of "the positive life," free of sickness and anxiety.[22]

Faith healing plays a central role in Sekai Kyūseikyō. The following conversation held with a devout teacher of the sect will reveal the teaching of this group regarding sickness and its cure:

Q. Will any disease yield to this treatment?
A. Yes, gradually. At present severe cases of cancer are not healed. It is possible that little by little, as we purify our souls, we will not need doctors.
Q. Are there cases of cancer being cured?
A. Yes.
Q. Is the faith healing method decided by the Founder or by the followers?
A. The principal method or doctrine does not change. It was decided by the Founder who acted in accordance with revelation.
Q. Could a follower receive the same revelation as the Founder?
A. There can be no comparison between them. The Founder was given a revelation which is not needed by the ordinary believer.
Q. How long does a treatment take?
A. A treatment takes longer if a person is deep in sin or needs more purification. However, treatments are always positive, even if a person does not believe.
Q. Are there set prayers for healing? . . .
A. Divine light is channelled through my body as an instrument of healing. It takes about fifteen minutes.[23]

Testimonies to physical healing through faith in the Worship Object and repetition of the prayer, *Namu Myōhōrengekyō,* make up a large body of the Sōka Gakkai newspaper and monthly picture graphic. Issued three times weekly, the *Seikyō Shinbun* (Holy Teaching News) carries principally news of Sōka Gakkai activities, sermons by the president, and testimonials. In the month of November, 1964, among the testimonials to faith healing were (1) report of the cure of infantile paralysis in the eight-year-old oldest son of the Hasegaya family of Nakano, Tokyo, (2) cure of diabetes and restoration to health of emaciated Mrs. Yuriko Sunaga (age 34) of Tokyo, (3) complete recovery from an intestinal ulcer and heart murmur by a member of the young woman's team in the gymnastic events of the Sōka Gakkai Olympics, her maladies having been attributed to her former relation to the Christian Church and then to Tenshō Kōtai Jingūkyō, "false religions," (4) the cure of stomach ulcer in sixty-one-year-old Fujita of Shirataka, and (5) release from convulsions for young Kazuyo Aoki of Hachiōji near Tokyo.

One convert reported (in the *Seikyō Shinbun,* August 26, 1960) that scars from the atomic bomb had been removed through faith in the Worship Object, but the majority of "healings" have been release from psychosomatic illnesses such as headaches or stomach pains.

Whenever it appears that the magic of healing does not work there is always the explanation, "You don't have enough faith." A woman, age 31, who was suffering with gall bladder trouble, asked Toda in a public meeting if she would get well. "How long have you been a believer?" was the teacher's first question. She answered, "One month." Then Toda asked, "How many converts," "Two," she confessed. "That kind of faith is no faith at all," he chastised her. Then Toda told how Nichiren had extended his own mother's life by four years, but only through the magic of an amulet, and not with medicines. The power was in his faith. He told her that through her faith in the power of the Worship Object she could get well. But since the proof of one's faith is in his works of converting others, she was like a man expecting wages without working for them.

Material Gain. Outside a temple in Okinawa there has recently been installed a billboard which reads, "Rewards for Belief: Healing from Sickness, Harmony in the Home, Business Success, Safety on the Sea, Protection from Traffic Accidents." The latter "benefit" appears to be a concession to the recent traffic boom.

Success in business, in the highly competitive economic whirl of modern Japan, seems to be the most luring bait offered to prospective converts. And Sōka Gakkai, of all the popular religions in Japan today, has capitalized most on this appeal. In fact, in the handbook for the indoctrination of converts (*Shakubuku Kyōten*) such religions as Tenrikyō are ridiculed for emphasis upon works of service to humanity which, according to Sōka Gakkai, reduces to a state of poverty any believer who takes the teaching seriously.

As Toda promised in the quotation cited above, a true believer never goes hungry; and if he is hungry, this is a sure sign that he is not a true believer. Little attempt is made to explain the connection between faith and business acumen; the usual approach is to call upon the prospective convert to turn everything over to the Worship Object, and he can be confident that through some mysterious working of fate good fortune will begin to come his way. The following testimony taken from the *Seikyō Gurafu* (Holy Teaching Graphic), given by an Ōsaka businessman, age 39, is a typical example:

I took up my father's business to become second in line. I've been managing the business for the past ten years. In 1956, after I had been a believer for two years, just as the business was beginning to get along, I lost both factory and home by fire. Not only that, but the insurance on them had expired. That was enough to give a man a headache. But Toda scolded me, "The fate which you inherited—to be poor—is being broken. If you can't stand up now, it means that you haven't much faith." Then I lost a child and at last my eyes were opened; that spurred me into action! I turned everything over to the Worship Object. In half a year not only had the factory been rebuilt, but in addition a new factory was put up in Nagoya. In the process of making plastic products we became the special factory for a top electric machine manufacturer, as well as acquiring a franchise to export a pure-water-bacteria-exterminating machine. Just the other day, I returned from a business trip to Taiwan, and at present we are thinking of building new factories. I guess I have a middle- or small-business man's disposition, but I never thought any bigger than having enough to eat and a little spending money. But now I've changed my way of thinking until I've decided that both my employees and I must prosper. My gastric ulcers and sciatica have been cured, my weight has increased from about 100 to 139 pounds, until friends call me the "little tank." All of my family are now believers. In whatever I do I give it all I've got and doors open.

The testimony of another businessman, who decided to try Sōka Gakkai from a motive similar to the one just quoted, reveals somewhat more specifically some practical aspects of membership in Sōka Gakkai which might contribute to business success:

I had had to take over the business after the war and wasn't really able to manage it. Sword broken, arrows spent, I was caught in the vicious circle of my own incompetence and the inflation which occurred after the war. In May, 1953, I went to Nagoya on business. There I had my palm read, and was told that in front of me was a huge lake, while behind me there was a steep cliff. This was my situation exactly. Then a friend, E., who was a member of Sōka Gakkai, told me of how joining the society had helped him in business. In gratitude for what the Worship Object had done for him he began to spread this wonderful mercy to others, and had acquired great merit. So he had come to win me. He told me that it was because I was a member of the Zen Denomination that all this misfortune had befallen me. The punishment of the three-evils and the four-evils had come upon me. If I continued in this way it was certain that I would be reborn in the world of the beasts. I was worshipping scraps of paper. . . . If only I would take the Worship Object and believe, all my problems would be solved. In the society all are comrades. Comrades help each other. With the cooperation of comrades my business would improve. Among comrades there is no worry about payments overdue. I was ready to grasp at a straw. At the age of 34 I had had to assume the responsibility for more than thirty employees. I was ready to try anything to make a go of it.

To be fair to Sōka Gakkai it must be added that such temporal benefits as have been described above are not the only benefits promised to the devout. The greatest benefit, of course, is the promise that a believer can attain the state of buddhahood in the present life. But, while contending that attaining this state is the greatest merit which a believer can acquire, it is constantly promised that definite, material proofs that one has attained the highest state will be given in this life, and that if such proofs are not manifest it is proof that the person has not yet attained the state of buddhahood.

4. The religion is aimed at filling the sociopsychological need for "belonging."

Perhaps the outstanding reason for the success of Risshō Kōseikai (chief rival of Sōka Gakkai, both of which are in the Nichiren Buddhist tradition), which was able to win over a million followers in the first twenty years from its formation in 1938, is to be found in the practice called *hōza* (group conferences), which is in continuous progress at the Tokyo headquarters and at local branches (totalling 89 throughout the country) every day of the year. Daily attendance at the conference in the main hall at Suginami-ku, Tokyo, is said to average more than ten thousand. These figures are not difficult to believe if one has ever visited headquarters. The author had the opportunity of entering into a *hōza* circle, where we were divided into groups of twenty, squatting on the mat floor knee-to-knee listening to the advice of a leader. It was a surprise to hear the mundane nature of the questions asked and the irrelevance to religion or faith in both questions and answers. These sessions are more in the nature of family or personal counseling. The leader, whether through experience or training, is able to offer common-sense advice on family problems, husband-wife quarrels, proper conduct on the train, child rearing, and a number of related subjects. To the participants (mostly women of middle age) the *hōza* offers an opportunity for sharing common everyday problems with persons of the same background and status (even at the headquarters the groups are divided with respect to one's home residence). The answer to a problem is not always given by the leader. Sometimes another housewife in the group offers a helpful suggestion, or one is relieved from the embarrassment of presenting his own delicate problem because another has brought a similar one before the group. Some of the principles of group dynamics are in full swing here.

One of the chief concerns of Risshō Kōseikai is that the believer become aware of the *uji-gami* (the clan kami) to whom he is historically and spiritually related. The individual must find where he "belongs," or he has no channel through which to appropriate the benefits of faith. Much time and effort are spent in tracing ancestry and titular deities.

The discussion meeting (*zadankai*) is the means by which Sōka Gakkai establishes group identity on the part of her converts. Breaking the membership down into small "squads" of about twenty, the trained leaders are able to deal with personal problems in semimonthly meetings in the friendly atmosphere of the squad leader's living room. A great deal of time is devoted to hearing the testimonies of members who have been helped in business or healed of some sickness, or enabled to solve some family problem. Each of the members wears his badge and carries his scriptures and *Shakubuku Kyōten* (Manual on Forced Conversions) in the familiar black zipper case. In referring to each other as "comrade" there is a familiarity and sense of "belonging" which boosts the individual's morale.

The son of our cleaning woman (who is a member of Sōka Gakkai) remarked when he returned home after a trip on a Sōka Gakkai chartered train with his mother to the head temple, "Society members are all swell, aren't they!" He had caught the spirit.

Another aspect of the sense of belonging is the feeling of being wanted and needed. Whereas the established religions in Japan seem to have developed a professional group of leaders who are entrusted with the business of running the religion, popular sects have stressed the importance of the layman. In most of these religious groups there are no priests or "professionals" of any kind. In most of them (with the exception of Tenrikyō and Konkōkyō) there is no institution of any kind to train professional leaders. In Ōmoto there are at present a total of only twenty-eight "missionary envoys," and there is no special school to train them; yet there were reported, in 1960, to be 5,379 "evangelists" who carried on the propaganda of this sect in their spare time while continuing regular employment in their respective occupations.[24] Teachers of the P.L. ("Perfect

Liberty") Kyōdan are professionals who must not engage in side work, but their salaries are fixed at a meager yen 5,000 (with an additional yen 5,000 for wife according to the 1960 report), and the teacher must be ready to move lock, stock, and barrel on forty-eight hours' notice from headquarters. The period of training for leaders of popular religions is negligible when compared to preparation for the Christian ministry, for instance. Most of them do not require a high school diploma, and the majority give a teacher's status to one who has taken special instruction for a few weeks or months.

The priests of the Nichiren Shō Denomination with which Sōka Gakkai is affiliated as a lay organization are trained over a long period of time in the traditional manner of Buddhism, but Sōka Gakkai leaders are nonprofessional laymen. The organization of Sōka Gakkai is especially designed to employ the maximum of lay leaders to the fullest. Each squad, company, district, and regional chapter has its lay leader who has received some kind of special instruction (but no remuneration) from the headquarters in Tokyo.

To use a maximum number of lay leaders and to make for more efficient running of the organizational machinery, Sōka Gakkai is divided into a number of relatively independent departments. Among these are the youth department, the student department, the women's department, the finance department, the culture department, publications, and so on.

The frequent mass gatherings of Sōka Gakkai serve as morale boosters. It is reported that 100,000 spectators and 14,000 performers jammed the National Stadium in Tokyo for the second "Culture Festival" staged by Sōka Gakkai immediately after the close of the Tokyo Olympic Games, on November 8, 1964. A Junior Fife-and-Drum Corps composed of 200 girls marched in review. The Young Men's Division presented 2,500 members in precision gymnastic routine. A mixed chorus of 12,000 voices sang the pep songs of the faith. Over one thousand guests including Prince Mikasa (brother to the Emperor), ambassadors, and Japanese cabinet members looked on in dumbfounded admiration. Some remarked that it was "better than the Olympics."

The requirement to win another to the faith before the believer can expect to reap any reward for his own faith serves a dual function. Not only does this activity of winning others help to make the individual's own faith more secure, it also gives him a feeling that he is useful and an integral part of the "team."

5. The religion offers a channel of release for youthful vigor.

The P. L. Kyōdan has specialized in a program for young men. The headquarters in Ōsaka is an extensive estate where one can "get back to nature." On the grounds there is a beautiful 18-hole golf course, tennis courts, and baseball diamonds. The daily pattern of *asamairi* (morning visit-worship) from 6:00 to 7:30, in which the believer visits the meeting hall for a period of worship, silent meditation, counseling, followed by breakfast which is served by the women of the group, is obviously designed for employed people who do not have family responsibilities.

Seichō no Ie attracts young unmarried girls through its emphasis on cultural activities—folk dancing, flower arrangement classes, development of the art of the tea ceremony, drama clubs, premarital counseling.

Young people who have grown up in the agnostic climate of postwar Japan are made to feel, in these popular religions, that religion has a place in their lives, albeit a subjective, utilitarian place. Japan's lonely youth, who are struggling to find some kind of personal identity in the mad whirlpool of entrance examinations, crowded schools, live-in employment, are attracted to the active youth programs of such groups as Sōka Gakkai where they can find a release for their pent-up energy in mass field days, music festivals, debate meetings, and where they are made to feel that each individual is a vital unit of the organization.

Though there are no "hymns" in this sect, Sōka Gakkai makes wide use of rousing "pep" songs, many of which were popular tunes among soldiers during the Second World War. In the youth rallies these songs are led with a gusto and vigor which remind one of a pep rally before a football game, or of the "warm-up" before an old-fashioned "revival meeting." The theme song of Sōka Gakkai would have to be heard to be fully appreciated for its appeal to youth, but the words themselves are revealing:

> As the blossoms fall to the ground in a night
> Let me fall under the wind that lifts this flag.
> You'll lose your life, one way or other,
> But a man goes down in glory.

> A man never shows his tears, and yet
> We weep inside when our spirits meet.
> We exchange a look across the wine cups,
> And red blood fills our veins.

> Though a pistol's pressed against my heart
> Not one step back I'd make.
> There is only one road for a man to travel—
> Eyes up, East, to the dawn!

The attraction of Sōka Gakkai to housewives cannot adequately be explained short of probing the various anxieties and longings of the individual believers themselves, but no one watching three thousand of these women stepping lively in parade, or dancing some traditional Japanese folk-dance in the annual Autumn Field Day, can help being struck by their sense of unity and the similarity of expression on their faces. These middle-aged women, who were rushed from elementary school immediately into employment or motherhood, seem to have found in Sōka Gakkai a second chance at the beauty and thrill of youth. Joining the study sessions of the society on an equal footing with college students, they feel they have also been given a second chance at an education. Sōka Gakkai, to them, is salvation from a mean, servile social order where a woman was taught to serve man three times in her life: her father, as a child; her husband, when she married; and her son, in her old age. In Sōka Gakkai, she, too, is an individual for whom the "value life" of happiness is possible of achievement.

6. The religion relieves the individual of the necessity of personal moral decision, and brings consolation that the believer is religious without demanding radical inner change.

To view this point in its proper perspective it would be necessary to examine the teachings of all the popular faiths, especially with respect to their view of man. Whether a radical inner change is demanded of the believer or not will depend upon what the religion considers to be the innate basic nature of man. Most popular religions take an optimistic view of man. Man is basically good. He may be warped or misled, he may be the victim of his past mistakes and misdeeds, but the essential thing for man to do in order to attain salvation is to rediscover his true basic nature.

To view man as a sinner, in the Christian meaning of the term, is to view man in relation to the Christian concept of God. Without the concept of a Creator-God in whose likeness man is created it cannot be expected that a religion will have a keen appreciation of sin and moral wrong.

These general observations are substantiated upon examination of the concept of man held by the various popular religions.[25] In Tenrikyō, for instance, there is no concept of man as sinner. It is true that man has allowed his heart to be covered with "dust"—desire, pride, etc. When a man's heart is covered with "dust" his body becomes weak and sickness ensues. Sickness itself is a sign that one has allowed "dust" to collect in his heart. By one's own effort he is able to sweep his heart clean and live the cheerful life. If one is not physically ill it is a sign that his heart is free of "dust," and there should be nothing to concern him. It is only when one is sick or troubled that he needs to renew his efforts to rid his heart of the "dust."

In Konkōkyō there is no place for the idea that a man can be alienated from God. There is no word to correspond to the concept of sin. There is no great differentiation between God and man. The founder himself is called the Living God Konkō, and belief is the means by which one becomes god. The idea of sin and punishment is not taught, but believers are reminded that through trust they will receive divine favor.

Seichō no Ie definitely teaches that sin does not exist, just as sickness and death are also unreal. Twisting the Christian Scriptures to fit his own ideas, Taniguchi (especially in his work *Seimei no Jissō*) claimed that God could not create sinful men. He makes Paul to say, instead of "There is none righteous; no, not one," rather, "There is no sinner; no, not one."

As for Sōka Gakkai, man's status is clearly stated. If a man worships the Worship Object he will be saved; if he does not worship the Worship Object he is damned. Repentance is not called for; a change of heart, regret for misdeeds, any attempt to right a wrong committed—these are not mentioned. Acceptance of the Worship Object and a faithful repetition of the prayer, *Namu Myōhōrengekyō,* are the sole requirements for fulfilling man's mission on earth. Disbelief brings physical, material, and eternal misfortune. Belief brings fortune and happiness (the words are interchangeable in Japanese) in the world, and promise of a better existence in the next.

Religious belief, as described above, is treated by most popular religions as a kind of magic formula which, when put to work for man, makes everything come out right. There seems to be very little moral instruction in any of these religions, with the possible exception of Konkōkyō.[26] Those like Risshō Kōseikai and Tenrikyō, which offer counseling on moral problems, have little doctrinal basis for their moral teachings, but take the accepted social pattern as standard. Eclectic sects such as Seichō no Ie have adopted the Sermon on the Mount.

The important thing to the average member of popular religions is that he is not held responsible individually for making his own moral decisions. In Sōka Gakkai important decisions are talked over at discussion meetings and the decision of the leader is taken as final. (This has been the traditional pattern in counseling in Japan.) But the member of Sōka Gakkai is not plagued by a continuous confrontation with moral choices as is the Christian, because religion to him is not so much a *way* of life in which he is enjoined to walk daily as it is a *key* to happiness which magically opens doors that have previously been locked to him.

To many Japanese the popular religions have afforded an opportunity to align oneself with religious faith again without any inward spiritual change. The great numbers converting to Sōka Gakkai do not represent new conversions to Buddhism. Most of these new members were nominal Buddhists. But, to them, Buddhism had lost all meaning and relevance except as it was vaguely connected with the burying and memorial services for the dead. Sōka Gakkai now offers these nominal Buddhists a living, active Buddhism, which they, as traditional Buddhists, feel they can be proud to claim. It is true that some of these were converted from another sect or denomination of Buddhism, but there is still a vague connection in the mind of the believer with the sense of pride in the fact that traditional Buddhism and the original teachings of Gautama, the Buddha, have come alive again. Some are consciously proud, as a friend of ours obviously was, that at last the Japanese Buddhists are beginning to know what Buddhism is all about.

7. The religion consciously encourages a sense of continuity with familial and national heritage.

Japan has been traditionally Buddhist. At least this is the way the average man on the street puts it. Buddhism has long since shaken the adage "alien" with which Christianity is labeled to this day. Most Japanese claim Buddhism as their religion, at least when a census is taken. Consequently, a revival in Buddhism in Japan is tantamount to a recovery of the national identity; not unlike what has happened in Burma since she gained her independence.

On the other hand, the gods of native Shintō are not to be treated lightly. Thus, some popular religions, such as Risshō Kōseikai, have encouraged continued veneration of ancestors, and even Sōka Gakkai, which aggressively renounces Shintō, in recent years has had to make concessions with regard to the treatment of ancestral tablets (objects of veneration in Shintō).

The basic social unit in Japan has traditionally been the *ie* ("house," or "family"). While Christianity has often been criticized as being divisive, with its insistence upon the responsibility of the individual before God, Japanese religions of Shintō and Buddhism have always fitted into this family structure. Popular religions, too, have indicated the importance which they place on the family as the lowest divisible unit in the society by refusing to number believers by individuals but insisting upon registering them as *setai* (family units). In a society such as

Japan where individual decision and opinion—especially by an inferior member of the family—has not been regarded, it is very difficult for one to stand alone in his religious convictions. The popular religions have realized this and have taken measures to win converts by families instead of by individuals.

Yet no religious group in Japan has caused more friction in family religion and traditions than Sōka Gakkai. In this respect Sōka Gakkai does not fit the pattern of religions in Japan, and for this express reason it has incurred the wrath of all organized religious groups in the country. Because of its uncompromising belief that all other religious faiths are false, and that false belief is the cause of all individual and public misfortunes, Sōka Gakkai is inherently opposed to familial and religious tradition in Japan outside its own faith. Nevertheless, this faith is not unsympathetic with the basic desire on the part of the Japanese to maintain the ties with tradition. It is here that we can see the real necessity for the wedding of Sōka Gakkai and the Nichiren Shō Denomination. The lay society as a "new religion" would have failed to appeal to this emotional demand for a traditional religious heritage. It is here, too, that Sōka Gakkai's exclusivism is beginning to show signs of breaking down, with an increasing trend to make concessions to traditional family religious observances and customs which are basically opposed to the teachings of Sōka Gakkai.

Sōka Gakkai is nationalistic. We must reach this conclusion in spite of the group's own claim to the universality of its faith and recent foreign mission activity. Whether it is "militaristic" or "fascist" as some critics claim is a question for later, more specific study (though it seems that this is a superficial criticism based primarily upon observation of the skillful organizational technique of the society). But it cannot be denied that Sōka Gakkai members are intensely proud of their own nationality. One member informed me that the reason why I was privileged to come and live in Japan was because of some merit I had stored up in a previous existence.

A basic doctrine of Sōka Gakkai is that Japan is the country where the "Vulture Peak" (of Gautama Buddha) is to be established in the last days, and from here the saving teaching that all men can attain buddhahood in this life is to be promulgated to the ends of the earth.

It is significant, too, that in the Nichiren Shō Denomination, Nichiren is exalted to the status of Buddha and is proclaimed as the Great Worship Object of all people. No foreign gods (such as Gautama Buddha) are worthy objects of faith for man in the present dispensation.

Where this nationalistic spirit will lead the Sōka Gakkai remains to be seen. Ultimately it will probably be the impetus for a movement on the part of this sect to take over the government. Already this aspect of Sōka Gakkai's underlying purpose has been manifested in its political activity. But this is a subject for another chapter.

I will be the pillar of Japan.
I will be the eyes of Japan.
I will be the great vessel of Japan.

(Nichiren)

三章 **JAPAN'S
BUDDHIST PROPHET**

Buddhism in the World

Buddhism is one of the three great living world religions. With a
history of 2500 years it has come down uninterrupted to the
present day. Like Christianity and Islam, Buddhism has proved
to be a *bond* which unites people of widely different racial origin
and cultures. In this sense Buddhism is one of the three universal
religions of mankind. But Buddhism has an even deeper dimension of universality than the linear dimension of history: from
its inception Buddhism has had a consciousness of its universal
mission to all men. The very heart of Gautama's enlightenment
was compassion, and for forty years he denied himself the fruits
of his own experience in order that he might share it with others.

What is Buddhism? Any attempt to describe it runs the risk
of becoming like the proverbial description of the elephant by
the blind men. A. K. Reischauer, in his book *Japanese Buddhism,*
looks upon Japanese Buddhism as "more like a junk shop where
one can find almost anything—good, bad, and indifferent." To
another scholar Buddhism appears not as a theology or a philosophy or a community, but as "a psychology which has the character and authority of religion."[1]

The legacy of Hinduism in Buddhism is perhaps the first key
with which to unlock the storehouse of this religious faith of 150
million, which extends in influence to a population of at least
772 million people—in Ceylon, Burma, Thailand, Cambodia,
Laos, Tibet, China, Korea, Outer Mongolia, and Japan. Though
Buddhism was more of a reaction against Hinduism than a development or extension of this ancient Indian religion, the influence
of the older religion is significant.

The interaction of Hinduism and Buddhism may be seen in
the following areas:

1. Ritual. The Hindu practice of sacrifice and coercion of the gods was repudiated by Buddhism as being naïve. The idea of castes and the moral superiority of some people over others was considered to be nonsense. Later, however, syncretism with Hindu thought began to corrupt the primitive Buddhism until Buddhist thought became absorbed into the amorphous mass of Hinduism. Hindu magic, rites, belief in bhakti (religious devotion), and sexual symbolism (which was so abhorrent to Gautama) were incorporated in later Buddhism. The legacy of ritual from Hinduism is manifest in Tantric Buddhism, which developed in Tibet and Mongolia.

2. The Gods. The Vedic (referring to the four *Vedas* from which Hindu thought evolves) concept of deity was henotheistic; i.e., in a pantheon of gods there was alternate belief in different gods as highest. Traditionally the gods were considered to be thirty-three in number and were divided into three groups—the celestial gods, the atmospheric gods, and the terrestrial gods. Primitive Buddhism denied the existence of any god, except in a temporal sense. Gods existed only as man exists, momentarily. But the position of the gods was less favorable than that of man because only in the world of desire and suffering—i.e., man's world—was there any hope of salvation. There is no Creator-God in Buddhism; no highest or everlasting god with divine power. This concept differs radically from the Hindu point of view.

3. Asceticism. In Hinduism asceticism was practiced to gain power over the forces of nature. In primitive Buddhism magical powers were considered hindrances to the achievement of true enlightenment. But renunciation of the world became essential for spiritual insight in Buddhism as it developed.

4. Intellectual Orientation. In this sphere Buddhism is no different from other Hindu philosophies—i.e., salvation is only attainable through knowledge (but this does not mean academic knowledge). For Buddhism and Hinduism, knowledge is the prerequisite to right living. Ignorance is a disease which hides one's true, healthful self. The cause must be known in order to effect the cure. The final ends of the chain of causation—old age, death—are eradicated through knowledge.

5. Stages of Religious Growth. As with Hinduism, Buddhism sets up a vast scheme of steps and stages in religious maturity. Gautama's enlightenment was his insight into the fact not that man *is* but that man *is becoming*.

6. Incarnation. Primitive Buddhism rejected the Hindu idea of a savior (*avatār*). Gautama said, "No one else can be a lamp for you." But at the heart of the Enlightenment was compassion, and the result, in Buddhism, was the development of the concept of the bodhisattvas—those who did not leave the realm of *rūpa-dhātu* (pure form world) so that they might help others to achieve enlightenment. The development of this idea occurred chiefly in the Mahāyāna (Greater Vehicle) school of Buddhism, which spread to China, Korea, and Japan. The Hinayāna (Lesser Vehicle, or Therevada) school which developed in Ceylon, Burma, and Thailand became characterized as cloistered Buddhism.

7. Other-Worldliness versus This-Worldliness. Hinduism had attempted to get beyond the veil of this world of impermanence and transcience to the transcendental permanent "other" world. The solution appeared in the merging of the one with the All. Behind and within this temporal world a trans-temporal world was recognized. Buddhism went much further. Primitive Buddhism denied any permanence in man at all. Man is becoming. This concept of Buddhism (known as radical pluralism) analyzes everything into its immediate constituents, and even these immediate constituents were seen to exist only for an infinitesimal lapse of time. Buddhism, as such, is a kind of humanism; man is the arbiter of his own self. At this point Buddhism makes a clean break with Hinduism and with all Indian religions.

Japanese Buddhism

Japanese Buddhism must be viewed in the larger perspective of universal Buddhism.

Mahāyāna Buddhism, less rigorous in doctrine and practice than primitive Buddhism, was the vehicle for the transportation of this faith out of India and north to Central Asia, China, Korea, and finally, in A.D. 552, to Japan. Gautama, the Buddha, had become deified, and the concept of bodhisattva became a subordinate deity who offered enlightenment or salvation to all men. On the way north and east this Buddhism collected a rapidly growing coterie of gods of non-Buddhistic origin. Mahāyāna matured mainly in the free religious atmosphere of T'ang Dynasty China when Confucianism was temporarily in eclipse. It was a more emotional and less philosophical faith than the Hīnayāna form, which demanded detachment from life and even monasticism.

Buddhism was introduced to Japan through Korea. Japanese monks of the Nara period (710-784) sought out the new faith in the T'ang capital and brought it back to Japan. Chinese monks also journeyed to Japan bringing new doctrines. At first the sophisticated foreign dogma remained a religion for a narrow priesthood and had little effect on the morality and outlook of the people. The common man interpreted the Buddhist pantheon as being manifestations of their native Shintō kami. At times Buddhism was adopted as a new kind of magic, at others it was used to satisfy the prestige desires of the young state, or it was espoused as a weapon in the power struggle between clans.

By the time of the great regent Shōtoku Taishi (593-622), the Japanese had gained a better understanding of Buddhism and it began to be promoted by the state. The Kegon sect and the *Kegon Sūtra* had great success in Nara, the capital. Emperor Shōmu built the greatest metallic image of Buddha (*Vairocana*) ever cast, and dedicated it in 754.

With Tendai and Shingon (esoteric) Buddhism, imported from China during the Heian period (794-1185), Buddhism became nationalistic and eclectic, merging with Shintō.

The Kamakura period (1185-1333) witnessed a violent reaction to the formalism of Tendai and Shingon, and popular sects with distinctive Japanese characteristics (Shin, Nichiren, and Zen) began to develop and found a warm reception among the common people.

The rise of new sects of Buddhism in Japan has usually been characterized by a movement toward orthodoxy to discover the essence of the true Buddhist faith. In fact, one may comment that every major reform in Japanese Buddhism has been in the direction of "orthodoxy" with the overall purpose of simplifying the faith and making it more palatable to the common man.

Hōnen's call in 1175 when he wrote his essay, the *Senchakushū* (Selections), was for a faith which would answer the needs of the common man, not for any radical break with Buddhist tradition. His emphasis on the "Pure Land" and the Original Vow of Amida Buddha was, as with Genshin and Ryōnin before him, an attempt to epitomize the essentials of the faith in a form simple enough for the common man to understand. Fed up with the impotency of ritual and form which had shackled Japanese Buddhism—especially through the influence of the effeminate Heian court—he discovered two roads to salvation, the "way of difficult practice" and the "way of easy practice." But it was the latter way, the easy way, which he opened to the people when he preached that salvation could be had through complete reliance upon the "other power" (*tariki*) of Amida.

Shinran (1173–1262), a disciple of Hōnen, took the refining process to its logical limit, claiming that if a faith response on the part of man to Amida's vow to save all mankind was efficacious, as Hōnen claimed, then it did not in the end depend upon the effort of man (*jiriki*) at all. Even the recitation of the *Namu Amida Butsu* (Hail to Amida Buddha), called the *Nembutsu,* which Hōnen enjoined his disciples to intone as often as possible, was not, for Shinran, the primary factor in man's salvation. Faith was the one essential requirement, and even this faith was not man's effort but was imparted to him by the power of the Other. And faith was not a complex of difficult dogma and intellectualism; for, said Shinran, reversing the statement of his teacher Hōnen, "If even a good man can be reborn in the Pure Land, how much more so a wicked man!"[2] Himself taking a wife and eating meat, Shinran tore down the wall of separation between clergy and laity.

Nichiren, less than a century later, sought for a further simplification of the tradition and attempted to make the faith relevant to the man on the street. For him it was the truth revealed in the *Lotus Sūtra* which ultimately and effectually opens the way for man to break the endless chain of sufferings and realize the state of buddhahood. Substituting the name of this *sūtra* for the name of Amida Buddha he discovered the invocation or prayer, *Namu Myōhōrengekyō* (Hail to the Wonderful Truth of the *Lotus Sūtra*) to contain the essence of the truth sufficient to bring salvation.

Each of these reformers obviously drew on forerunners for his attempted penetration to the heart of true Buddhism. "Pure Land" Buddhism was not original with Hōnen, but finds its origin in China. Shinran amply acknowledged his debt to Hōnen. And Nichiren, ignoring and denouncing both of these forerunners, drew on the insights of Dengyō Daishi, who had introduced the teachings of the Chinese patriarch Tendai Daishi into Japan in the eighth century (A.D.). But each of the three claimed independence from any teacher and presented his own insight as the final truth which supersedes any previous revelation.

The recent revival of the Nichiren Shō Denomination of Nichiren Buddhism through the efforts of Sōka Gakkai is not a reformation in the same sense as the above. Hōnen, Shinran, and Nichiren, while claiming "orthodoxy" for their teachings, actually inaugurated new movements in Buddhism and initiated beliefs (a savior, faith, paradise) and practices (a simple prayer of faith in the "Name") which are alien to the primitive Buddhist faith. Sōka Gakkai is a lay movement in Buddhism; it is a well-planned and skillfully led program to enlist the laity in winning converts. It has inherited the passion of the father and saint of the faith, Nichiren, to give religion to the people in terms which they can understand and grasp. In this sense Sōka Gakkai is a bridge between traditional and popular religious sects; and this is perhaps the reason why, despite its own protest, it has often been listed among the "new religions" of postwar Japan.

Nichiren

Nichiren (called Nichiren Dai Shōnin, "The Great Holy One, Nichiren," by members of the Nichiren Shō Denomination) was without doubt the most controversial figure in Japanese Buddhism. A man of great intensity, his mind would not permit sidetracks. He was the Japanese Buddhist counterpart of the Hebrew prophet Amos.

Interestingly enough the parallel with Amos holds true at several points. Amos saw in natural calamities, social injustices, and political upheaval the imminence of the judgment of God about to be visited upon those who had abandoned the true faith. Nichiren interpreted a succession of natural disturbances—the terrible earthquake of 1257, the destructive hurricane of 1258, the famine and pestilence of 1259, and the political turmoil of the times—as punishment upon the nation for her neglect of the Buddhist Dharma. Amos warned of foreign invasion and the eventual collapse of the nation of Israel, a prophecy which was fulfilled; Nichiren, in 1261, predicted an invasion from a foreign power, which was realized in 1268 when the envoy of the Mongol army landed on Kyūshū. Amos and Nichiren alike were prophets in the original Hebrew meaning of the term—men who read the signs of the times in terms of their religious faith. And both were men of unswerving dedication to a single, unyielding ideal. Amos' message is summed up by a single metaphor which he used— the plumbline, which stood for the righteousness of God who judges and punishes man's unrighteousness. Nichiren summed up his own message with the invocation-prayer, *Namu Myōhōrenge-kyō*, which stood for the central truth of the *Lotus Sūtra*, giving man the only means of escape from the calamities of the period of the End of the Dharma.

From the age of twelve Nichiren devoted himself for twenty years to a search for the truth. Born in Kominato in what is now Chiba Prefecture, he entered the nearby Tendai monastery of Kiyozumi, but later traveled throughout Japan—to Kyōto, Nara, Ōsaka, and Mt. Kōya, where he studied the teachings of the traditional Buddhist sects of Gusha, Jōjitsu, Ritsu, Sanron, Kegon, and Shingon. It is said that he was driven away from the monastery on Mt. Hiei (Tendai Denomination) because of his radicalism. Finally he came to the conviction that the only true faith was Dengyō Daishi's teaching of the ultimate superiority of the *Lotus Sūtra* over all other *sūtras*. After having found this truth for himself he returned to his home to preach to the com-

mon people and to announce to all men that salvation can be
attained through the earnest recitation of one simple prayer which
he considered to be the essence of the Buddha's teaching in the
Lotus Sūtra: Namu Myōhōrengekyō. He was now 31 years of age.

From time to time Nichiren appeared at the military capital,
Kamakura, to admonish government officials with his "memorials." The first of these, the *Risshō Ankokuron* (On the establishment of the legitimate teaching for the security of the country),[3] was presented to the authorities in 1261, condemning the
government for not keeping the Buddhist Dharma, and prophesy-
ing the imminence of foreign invasion as a consequence of the
nation's infidelity. As a result of this denunciation of the government officials Nichiren was banished to Izu Peninsula for a
period of two years, but eventually was pardoned on February
12, 1264.

After his return from banishment Nichiren gave no indica-
tion that he had repented of his former tirades against the government. On the contrary, his invectives grew even bolder, until
he announced to the people who would listen to him on the
streets of Kamakura that the Regent Saimyōji was in hell and
the current Regent Tokimune was preparing to follow him. This
brought down the full wrath of the government upon his neck
and he was sentenced to death. His execution was stayed, however, and he was sentenced instead to exile on Sado Island in
the Japan Sea. His deliverance from the hand of the executioner
on September 12, 1268, on the beach near Kamakura called
Yuigahama, is referred to as Nichiren's *Tatsunokuchi hōnan*
(suffering for the Dharma at Tatsunokuchi), and the prophet
himself considered it to be a miracle of divine intervention, accompanied by a lightning flash that stopped the executioner's
sword in midair. Nichiren often wrote as if he considered that
his body had died that day and that it was his soul that was
exiled to Sado.[4]

During this three-year period of exile (1271-1274) Nichiren
wrote the two works, *Kaimokushō* (On opening the eyes) and
Kanjin Honzonshō (On the contemplation of the true Worship
Object), which form the basis of the doctrine of the faith today,

and also created the original Worship Object (an inscription on wood of the prayer, *Namu Myōhōrengekyō*) which the Nichiren Shō Denomination claims to be enshrined in the Worship Hall of Taisekiji. (A rival branch of Nichiren Buddhism, the Nichiren Denomination, maintains that Nichiren wrote the original inscription while in residence at Minobu and that this original is enshrined in their head temple at Minobu.)

On March 13, 1274, Nichiren returned to Kamakura, having received pardon for the second time, still undaunted and unwilling to recant. He memorialized the government for the third time in April, 1274. This time he was forced into retirement, and, being already 54 years of age, decided to set about establishing the "Vulture Peak" which Nichiren believed should be found in Japan. The "Vulture Peak" is the mythological locality, corresponding to Rajagriba in India, from which Gautama is said to have delivered the teaching of the *Lotus Sūtra*. Acquiring patronage from a lay devotee, Hakii, Nichiren established on Mt. Minobu the Kuonji Temple which later became the head temple of the Nichiren Denomination. Here he continued to write, producing, among others, the *Senjishō* and the *Hōonshō* which are included in the sacred writings of the Nichiren Shō Denomination, as well as over 230 letters still extant.

In 1280, according to the Nichiren Shō Denomination, Nichiren proclaimed his "basic intent": the manifestation of "The Great Worship Object of the Altar of the Basic Doctrine." This is, specifically, the moment in which Nichiren revealed his sacred inscription to his disciples and initiated them into its mystery as the quintessence of true Buddhism.

Nichiren died on October 13, 1282, at the age of 61, at the home of his patron, Uemondayū Munenaka Ikegami. His remains were removed to the temple at Mt. Minobu, but another temple was established at the place where he died, known today as Ikegami Honmonji.

Of the six immediate disciples of Nichiren to whom he entrusted the religious offices to be performed at his grave after his death, only Nikkō, according to the Nichiren Shō Denomination, was faithful to the commission of the master. Though the other denominations in the Nichiren tradition all contend that Nichiren had enjoined six among his eighteen disciples to take turns performing the duties of his grave and that Nikkō became disgruntled and left, Nichiren Shō possesses two documents (the *Minobu sōjō* and the *Ikegami sōjō*) which are presented as conclusive proof that Nichiren had selected Nikkō alone to be his successor.[5] These documents, needless to say, are denounced as spurious by other Nichiren denominations.

According to Nikkō, the other five disciples[6] repudiated the true teaching of Nichiren and were therefore not worthy to perform the offices of his grave. In addition, the lay patron of the faith at Mt. Minobu, Hakii, according to Nikkō, through compromise with the military government, was guilty of slandering the Dharma (*hōbō*), which is the "unpardonable sin" of Buddhism. Claiming to be following a final secret command to "search out the Vulture Peak" and build the altar, Nikkō with his disciples Nichimoku and Nikke left Mt. Minobu to establish Taisekiji near the present village of Fujinomiya in Shizuoka Prefecture. This new site at the foot of Mt. Fuji was believed to be "the site suitable to be the center of world Buddhism." Under the patronage of Nanjō, a devout lay follower, a temple-residence called the Godaibō was constructed, and Nikkō and his disciples established themselves here in October, 1290.

The Nichiren Shō Denomination, of course, contends that Nikkō brought with him to Mt. Fuji the bones of Nichiren, the true Worship Object (the sacred inscription), and all other important relics. Other denominations of Nichiren Buddhism, having studied pictures of the Worship Object installed at Taisekiji, say that it cannot be authentic. In acrimonious retort, Sōka Gakkai members, at a debate held in Otaru with priest-scholars of the Nichiren Denomination, declared the supposed remains of Nichiren which their rivals enshrined at Mt. Minobu to be bones of a horse![7]

Denominations of Nichiren Buddhism

Before the Second World War there were nine different denominations in the Nichiren tradition: Nichiren, Nichiren Saijōkyō, Nichiren Fuju-fuse, Nichirenkyō, Nichiren Kōmon, Nichiren Shugi Butsuritsukō, Nichiren Shō, Nichiren Hokke, and Nichiren Hon. Today there are reported to be forty-one different Nichiren denominations.[8]

The Nichiren Shō Denomination (*Nichiren Shō-shū*) claims that the succession has been handed down directly from Nichiren to the present 66th abbot of Taisekiji. Among these were Nikkō, Nichimoku, and Nichidō, the three patriarchs, and Nichiyū (9th abbot) and Nikkan (26th abbot) who are referred to as the "two intermediate flourishing teachers." Nikkan (1665-1726) wrote the important work *Rokkanshō,* and helped to establish the doctrine as it is known today. The 65th abbot died in November, 1959, and the 66th, Saint Nittatsu, was then installed as Abbot of Taisekiji.

The name of Nichiren Shō means "True Nichiren," or "Orthodox Faith of Nichiren." But the name has undergone constant change and did not settle on its present form until 1912. At first it was known as the Hokke Denomination, then later as the Nichiren Hokke Denomination or, simply, the Nichiren Denomination. In the early Meiji period the faith was known as the Nichiren Denomination: Kōmon Branch (that is, the Nichiren faith which follows the doctrine of Nikkō). Later the majority of this group took the name of Honmon (the faith of the Basic Doctrine). After a period when the government forced its identification with other Nichiren denominations the name Nichiren Denomination: Fuji Branch was adopted.

The Lotus Sūtra (in Sanskrit: *Saddharmapundarīka sutra*)

The classification of Buddhist *sūtras* and the elevation of the *Lotus Sūtra* to the ultimate rank was a mammoth task accomplished by a sixth-century (A.D.) Chinese priest, Chih-k'ai (538-597), who is known in Japan as Tendai Daishi (from the Chinese T'ien-tai, name of a mountain). The classification is an attempt to harmonize the voluminous and often contradictory *sūtras* of the Hīnayāna and Mahāyāna schools. In order to build this harmony Tendai divided the forty-year teaching ministry of Gautama into five periods, and, placing the various *sūtras* within this framework, he managed to maintain the authority of them all by claiming that they originated in the teachings given by Gautama himself, while, at the same time, elevating the position of the *Lotus Sūtra* and the *Nirvāna Sūtra* by placing these in the last period of Gautama's ministry.[9]

While Nichiren accepted Tendai's classification of the *sūtras* as interpreted to Japan by Dengyō Daishi (767–822), who had been sent to China in 804 to study under the seventh patriarch of the Tendai school, Myōraku (in Chinese, Miao-le), he interpreted it to mean not that the *Lotus Sūtra* was merely superior to all other *sūtras* but that it was given to replace them.[10]

Up to this point the various denominations in the Nichiren tradition are in agreement concerning the prophet's intention and teaching. It was with the interpretation of Nichiren's exegesis of the *Lotus Sūtra* itself that division occurred.

The *Lotus Sūtra,* called *Hokekyō* in Japanese, was in existence before A.D. 250,[11] but higher criticism reveals that it could not have been given by Gautama himself as the followers of Tendai and Nichiren claim. The *sūtra* is obviously a treatise written to defend the worship of Gautama as the primordial Buddha which had developed in Mahāyāna Buddhism, and to justify the origin of the Mahāyāna school.

The fact which third- and fourth-century Buddhism had to deal with was the rise of two distinct schools of interpretation of the Buddhist doctrine, the Mahāyāna and the Hīnayāna.

In the *Lotus Sūtra* Gautama appears not as a historical person (though he is known to have been born Siddhartha Gautama, an Indian prince of the Shākya clan at Kapilavastu in Nepal in the seventh century B.C. and to have died in 544 B.C.) but as a supernatural being from between whose eyebrows issues a ray of light which extends over 18,000 Buddha fields. The setting laid for the giving of this the Buddha's final teaching is the Vulture Peak. The Buddha falls into a trance. A great rain of divine flowers covers him, and four groups of hearers appear. The light ray shines from between his eyebrows and lights up the Buddha fields. Then follows a period of silence, the great rain of divine flowers, and now the ray travels eastward. When the Buddha awakes from his trance he explains the meaning of the rain and the ray of light.

This is clearly a defense for the development of Mahāyāna Buddhism. The first of the three periods of the Buddhist Dharma[12] is closed. With the new interpretation of Buddhism given by Nāgārjuna (Buddhist scholar who lived in the second century A.D. in India and wrote the *Mādhyamika Kārikā,* the text which became the basis of the "Intermediate" school of Mahāyāna), the horizon of the Buddhist faith had been extended. The ray which issued from between the eyebrows of the Buddha had reached to China. Those who spread the Dharma of the first period of the Buddhist Dharma are praised and a reward is promised them. A new representative for the second period of the Dharma is introduced, Yaku-ō (in Sanskrit:*Bhalshajyarāja*). Many monks are offended by this announcement (referring, no doubt, to the Elders of the Hīnayāna), but there are still 80,000 who remain faithful.

At this point there takes place a scene which Nichiren symbolically depicted in the famous inscription which is now the central object of worship in Nichiren Buddhism. A *stūpa* descends from heaven and before the eyes of the worshiping multitude the image of Gautama is seen to fuse itself with the image of Tahō (in Sanskrit: *Prabhūta-ratna*), a former Buddha. Numerous bodhisattvas are gathered around to witness this meeting, among them being some made famous by various sculptured triads of the Nara temples in Japan: e.g., Monju Bosatsu (*Manjushri*), Kannon Bosatsu (*Avalokiteshvara*), and Yakushi Nyorai (*Bhalshajyaguru*). How this scene is depicted symbolically in the Chinese characters of Nichiren's sacred inscription is described in a later chapter.

According to Nichiren's interpretation this event then prepares the way for the advent of the final period of the Dharma (*mappō*). Chapter 15 of the *Lotus Sūtra* marks a definite transition point in the *sūtra,* and scholars since Tendai Daishi have postulated various theories to explain the relationship of the first fourteen and the last fourteen chapters. Difference in interpretation of the relationship of the two halves of the *Lotus Sūtra* has resulted in sectionalism in Nichiren Buddhism, dividing the denomination into three groups: (1) the *itchi* branch—those who believe that the two parts agree and are equal; (2) the *shōretsu* branch—those who claim that the latter part is superior to the former; (3) and the "orthodox" branch (Nichiren Shō)—which, though it agrees in principle with the *shōretsu* branch, claims that there is a doctrine which is "beneath the letter" (the implied rather than the literal meaning) of the *Lotus Sūtra*.

Chapter 15 (*"Jūchi-yuijutsuhon"*)[13] describes multitudes of bodhisattvas, beyond number, pouring out of the chasms of the earth. At the head of them all is Jōgyō Bosatsu (in Sanskrit: *Vishistacāritra*). It is this bodhisattva who appears in the period of the End of the Dharma, the period of complete despair, to bring comfort to the multitude. And it is with this bodhisattva that Nichiren is identified.[14]

The *Lotus Sūtra* has been an important scripture in the development of Mahāyāna Buddhism as it spread to China, Korea, and Japan. Three principal translations into Chinese appeared: in A.D. 286 by Dharmerakcha, in 406 by Kumārajīva, and in 601 by Gnanagupta and Dharmagupta. The standard translation into Japanese is that of K. S. Fukagawa (1904).

According to the prophet Nichiren the *Lotus Sūtra* is the perfect, true, Wonderful Dharma. It is the mysterious Wonderful Dharma grasped first by the Buddha, Gautama, and then by the many buddhas of the ten quarters of the three worlds, from Buddha to Buddha, incapable of being understood by common man. There is no other way for man to know the Wonderful Dharma than to receive in faith the teaching of the Buddha. In chapter 2 of the *Lotus Sūtra* ("Hōbenbon") the Wonderful Dharma is explained as the Great Dharma which is the kernel of the various Dharma. It is the Dharma (or "truth") of the ten *nyoze* ("suchness")—the truth that all creation contains each of ten conditions which are interrelated: (1) all objects are of such form; (2) all objects are of such nature; (3) all objects are of such substance; (4) all objects are of such power; (5) all objects are of such activities; (6) all objects come from such causes; (7) all objects have such conditions; (8) all objects come to such effects; (9) all objects acquire such reward; (10) all objects begin and are completed in such ways.

According to Nichiren the basic meaning of the *Lotus Sūtra* was made clear by Tendai Daishi. It is the truth of *ichinensanzen* ("one [intent] thought—three thousand [worlds]"). Tendai Daishi said, "If in one mind there are ten worlds, and in one Dharma world also there are ten Dharma worlds, they are 100. In one world there are 1,000 varieties of worlds. These 3,000 are in one thought of the mind. If without thinking they do not cease, how much more do the 3,000 worlds exist when one thinks on them."[15]

The ten Dharma worlds are the worlds of: (1) hell, (2) hungry spirits, (3) beasts, (4) pandemonium, (5) humans, (6) heavenly beings, (7) those disciples who understand the Four Noble Truths of Gautama's original teaching,[16] (8) the enlightened, (9) the bodhisattva—those who seek enlightenment not only for self but also for others, and (10) the buddhas—those who have gained supreme enlightenment and have entered Nirvāna. At times some of these worlds are stronger than others and it seems as if the others do not exist; but the truth of the *Lotus Sūtra* is that they all eternally exist simultaneously.

Each of the above ten Dharma worlds contains all the others, making 100 worlds. Each of these 100 worlds in turn contains the ten *nyoze,* making a total of 1,000 worlds. Each of the 1,000 worlds exist in three varieties: (1) the world of the self which is made up of the five *skandhas*—form, feeling, perception, conformation, and consciousness; (2) the world of the other; and (3) man's habitat. Thus there are 3,000 worlds. That these 3,000 worlds all exist simultaneously is the truth expressed by *ichinensanzen.*

If not until the giving of the *Lotus Sūtra,* not until the "*Hōbenbon*" (chapter 2), were men able to attain to the buddha-world, then the buddha-world did not exist. If the buddha-world did not exist, then all the 3,000 worlds are denied. Therefore, it is necessary to understand the meaning of the "*Nyorai Juryō-hon*" (chapter 16) of the *Lotus Sūtra* to realize that the 3,000 worlds have existed simultaneously ("in one thought") from eternity and that this doctrine constitutes the basic meaning "beneath the letter" of the *Lotus Sūtra*.

The *Lotus Sūtra*, as stated above, divides into two parts, the first fourteen chapters and the last fourteen. It is the last part which reveals that the Buddha has existed from eternity, and, hence, it is the last part of the *Lotus Sūtra* which contains the basic doctrine. The first part is a reflection of the truth of the *ichinensanzen* which is at the base of the *sūtra*. It is like a footprint in the sand. The footprint is a testimony to the reality which made it. Therefore, the first part of the *Lotus Sūtra* is called, by members of the Nichiren Shō Denomination, the "footprint doctrine." When we move from the first part to the last part, the "footprint doctrine" is replaced by the "basic doctrine," and "the moon in the pond now becomes the moon in the heavens."

But this understanding of the meaning of the *Lotus Sūtra* is not immediately available to all. The teaching of the *ichinensanzen* is not made explicit in the basic doctrine of the *Lotus Sūtra*. It was Tendai Daishi who discovered the truth, but Nichiren alone was able to see the superiority of the "basic" over the "footprint" doctrine and thus interpret the unwritten truth behind the letter. In the *Hon'inmyōshō* Nichiren wrote:

> And he asked him saying, Tell me of the hidden truth, the Great Thing which lies beneath the letter of the *"Nyorai Juryōhon."* Answering he said, It is only the secret true Dharma. It must be hidden, must be hidden. That which is written by the *nirmāna buddha* of the first generation [Gautama] is the theory of ideation-only, built on reason.
>
> This understanding of the meaning of the basic doctrine of the *"Nyorai Juryōhon,"* which is based upon the theory of *ichinensanzen,* I call the maturation according to the letter. The truth beneath the letter is the Name of the Wonderful Dharma, which depends not upon performance of excessive works, but is apprehended directly through the Namu Myōhō-rengekyō.[17]

To summarize, the *Lotus Sūtra,* for Nichiren followers, contains six central teachings: (1) all men can attain buddhahood; (2) Buddha is eternal, without beginning or end; (3) Gautama's personal salvation guarantees the salvation of all; (4) Gautama prophesies that after his own demise all his teachings except the *Lotus Sūtra* will lose their efficacy; (5) the bodhisattvas are all assembled in the congregation in the sky above the Vulture Peak, and have pledged themselves to proclaim the Wonderful *Lotus Sūtra,* the chief of the bodhisattvas being Jōgyō Bosatsu, who was incarnated in Nichiren; (6) Jōgyō Bosatsu (Nichiren) will receive persecution and untold hardship, but eternal comfort and protection shall be given him and all who keep no more than the sacred prayer, *Namu Myōhōrengekyō.*

Otoko tōru michi tada hitotsu
Aoge higashi no akane-zora

There is only one road for a man to travel—
Eyes up, East, to the dawn!

(from the Sōka Gakkai theme song)

THE MARTYR
AND THE ORGANIZER

The Founder, Makiguchi

Sōka Gakkai (Society for the Creation of Value, the term *Gakkai* being widely used in academic circles in Japan to mean "study society") looks to a Tokyo elementary school principal, Tsunesaburō Makiguchi, as its founder. Born in Niigata Prefecture on June 6, 1871, the oldest son of Chōmatsu Watanabe, he was adopted into the Makiguchi family at the age of three. After finishing elementary school he went to Hokkaidō (the northern island) to complete his education. First he lived in Otaru but later graduated from the Normal School at Sapporo. He was retained as an instructor at his alma mater until he had prepared a manuscript of his studies in geography which he called *Shizen to Ningen to no Kankei* (The Relationship of Nature and Man). Eventually, at the age of 31, with a wicker basket full of manuscript, and hardly anything else, he took the inevitable road to Tokyo.

Though his work was clearly a sociogeographical study, since the word "social" was in ill-repute at this time Makiguchi's book was published (in 1903) by the Fuzanbō Publishing House under the title *Jinsei Chirigaku* (Geography of Life). This book contained the germ of Makiguchi's theory concerning the creation of value (*sōka*) which became the ideological foundation of Sōka Gakkai. His book *Kachiron* (Theory of Value) was published after his death under the editorship of Toda and was established as the theoretical premise of Sōka Gakkai.

The antecedent of the Sōka Gakkai of today was the Sōka Kyōiku Gakkai (Society for Education in the Creation of Value), formed in 1937 at a meeting of some sixty members in a restaurant in Azabu, Tokyo. Makiguchi was installed as president and Toda was made vice-president.

This group, reacting to the prevailing theory of education in the immediate prewar years, dedicated itself to a study of the purpose and goal of education. They concluded that the goal of education should be the attainment of happiness and that happiness consists in the creation and accruement of values. Education, according to them, should be the guide to the creation of values, and educators should be expected to give planned leadership to students in guiding them into the value-life of "beauty, benefit, and good," the three postulated values of the *Kachiron*. Only in this manner could a peaceful, secure life of happiness be achieved. It was a movement to rationalize education.

Though the group itself was small (claiming 3,000 members before World War II) it soon became apparent to the Japanese authorities that what these people stood for was in diametric opposition to the government-sponsored spiritual mobilization of the 1930's which gave special favor to Shintō, and it became increasingly difficult for the group to continue as a study organization. The use of the term *kyōiku* (education) in the name of the organization set them in open defiance of the policy of the Education Ministry for regimented education throughout the country. In turn this word was dropped from the title and affiliation with the Nichiren Shō Denomination of Buddhism was sponsored, it would seem, in an effort to escape government proscription.

According to Sōka Gakkai sources[1] Makiguchi had fallen under the influence of a fellow school principal in Tokyo, one Sokei Mitani, who was an ardent follower of Nichiren Shō. Convinced by this "logician" that his educational theories needed the support of religious belief, Makiguchi converted to the Nichiren Shō Denomination in 1928. But Nichiren Buddhism was no more popular with the war leaders than were unorthodox education theories. Not only did the Nichiren Shō Denomination take an unequivocal stand, refusing merger with other Nichiren denominations in spite of pressure from government officials, there was also the "Mandala Affair" in which the government took the position that the sacred inscription (Mandala) written by Nichiren and held sacred as the Worship Object by Nichiren groups was an open affront to the Emperor because of the degrading position given to the Emperor Ōjin (who ruled in the fourth century A.D.) and Amaterasu, the Sun Goddess, in the arrangement of the names in this inscription. Their names were given a position "between the legs," so to speak, of the characters spelling out the prayer, Namu Myōhōrengekyō.[2]

Makiguchi was finally forced to resign as principal of the Shinbori Elementary School, and the magazine which he had begun in 1941 (*Kachi Sōzō,* the Creation of Value) was suppressed in May, 1942, after only nine issues. Finally, on July 6, 1943, while stopping over in Shimoda, Makiguchi was arrested by the special police and subsequently was imprisoned, with twenty others of the group including Toda, on the charge of *lèse majesté.* The specific charge was that they had refused, on the basis of religious belief, to accept the *taima,* a talisman, from the Ise Shrine (Shintō). After a year and a half Makiguchi died, while still in prison, on November 18, 1944, at the age of 74.

The Organizing Genius, Toda

The real power behind the Sōka Gakkai movement was the inspired leadership of Makiguchi's protégé and second president of the organization, Jōsei Toda. Released in 1945 after two years in Sugamo Prison, Toda had two claims to the succession: he had been Makiguchi's most favored disciple, and he had suffered persecution for his loyalty to the group.

Toda was born in 1900 in Ishikawa Prefecture, but was reared in Hokkaidō. Prepared to teach in elementary schools, he too eventually found his way to Tokyo where, still only a youth of 21, he became a teacher at Nishimachi Elementary School where Makiguchi was then serving as principal. After three years, however, he gave up teaching and opened a private institute for tutoring students. During this period of private tutoring he published a textbook on mathematics called *Shidō Sanjutsu* (Guide to Mathematics) which sold over a million copies, and at the same time operated the Daidōsha Publishing House, specializing in the production of popular novels. Toda's decision to teach privately reflects the difficulty of the times in the educational world in Japan, but it is probably no coincidence that this new freedom also enabled him to devote more time to Makiguchi, for an intimate master-disciple relation had been established between the two almost from the moment of meeting.

Toda was the organizing genius behind the original society, and it was through his direction that various publications were begun. But all activity of Sōka Gakkai was halted in July, 1943, when Toda, along with Makiguchi and other leaders, was incarcerated.

Hearing while in prison that Makiguchi had died, Toda made a vow: "What do they mean, letting a man of the calibre of Makiguchi *Sensei* die in prison! All right, I'll show them! Toda will take up the mission of Makiguchi *Sensei*. Toda will see that the world hears this teaching!"[3]

Toda's dynamic motivation, unlike that of Makiguchi, was religious faith rather than educational principles. How far Makiguchi himself was successful in uniting his personal utilitarian philosophy with the principles of Buddhism is an enigma which perhaps never will be answered. But in Toda the educational principles laid down by Makiguchi and the world principles of the Nichiren Shō faith were completely fused. Toda became not only the proponent of his beloved teacher's ideas (in accordance with his prison vow), he became, in his own right, the prophet and chief propagator of the beliefs of the Nichiren Shō Denomination.

From January, 1946, Toda launched a movement for the resurrection of the group which he and Makiguchi had founded before the war, and set out to convert the nation to Nichiren Buddhism, as interpreted by the Nichiren Shō Denomination. He lectured on the *Lotus Sūtra* on various occasions, especially in the summer lecture sessions held every year at the head temple, Taisekiji. Subsequently the first general meeting of the group was held in the Kanda Education Hall, Tokyo, to commemorate the third anniversary of Makiguchi's death. This meeting is now taken to have been the first general assembly of the reorganized Sōka Gakkai.

Toda served as chairman of the Board of Directors of Sōka

Gakkai (not taking the title of president) until he resigned in November, 1949. The cause contributory to his resignation from the board was his indictment for fraud in connection with the management of the Tokyo Construction Credit Association of which he was head. This association declared bankruptcy during the inflation of 1949 and Toda was accused of embezzling funds by a man named Nakamura who had suffered a heavy loss. Toda never denied the accusation, but during the period when he was under police investigation he resigned his post as chairman of Sōka Gakkai and Yajima was appointed in his stead. Ultimately, however, charges against Toda were dropped, though the credit association was liquidated with the stipulation that Toda should refund thirty percent of the outstanding debt of yen 15 million by 1951.[4]

The formal beginning of Sōka Gakkai as it is known today was at a meeting on May 3, 1951, when Toda accepted the post as second president of the group with the words, "You must not give Toda a funeral if 750,000 family units have not been won. Throw my bones into the ocean off the coast of Shinagawa."[5]

Believing that the time for the dissemination of the doctrine (*kōsenrufu*) had come, Toda felt a divine commission to proclaim the truth as revealed by Nichiren. History is focused on the now, the Great Life of the Universe is lodged in the flesh of Nichiren (made immortal in this faith), in the magical prayer (called the *daimoku*) which Nichiren discovered, *Namu Myōhō-rengekyō,* and in the Worship Object (the sacred inscription called the *gohonzon*) which Nichiren wrote and left to be the central object of worship for all who would be saved in the dispensation of the End of the Dharma (*mappo*).

From this point on, the virulent drive to win converts was in progress. The publication of a monthly magazine, *Daibyaku Renge* (Great White Lotus), from July, 1949, and a weekly paper, *Seikyō Shinbun* (The Seikyo News), from April, 1951, gave impetus to the drive. By October, 1951, *Shakubuku Kyōten* (Manual on Forced Conversions, 445 pages) was off the press. In 1952, under the editorship of Toda, Sōka Gakkai published the collected works of Nichiren and his immediate disciple Nikkō in one volume and, giving it the name *Gosho* (Honorable Writings), elevated it to the rank of sacred scriptures for the Nichiren Shō Denomination. Toda's commentaries on the chief writings of Nichiren, on the *Lotus Sūtra,* his own *Seimeiron* (Theory of Life), and his edition of Makiguchi's *Kachiron* (Theory of Value), in 1953, are testimony to the indefatigable zeal which he dedicated to the propagation of this religious faith. He lectured at the general meetings of Sōka Gakkai and at other special mass lecture gatherings. His keen administrative ability, charismatic personality, and bellicose spirit, his struggle up through the ranks by sheer hard work, his aggressiveness and masculinity coupled with a keen sensitiveness, a sense of humor, and an astute mind—all these qualities added up to "charisma" and an irresistible leader. He was the kind of man postwar, insecure, disillusioned Japan could follow.

On March 1, 1958, on the occasion of the dedication of the Great Lecture Hall at Taisekiji, Sōka Gakkai announced that Toda's goal of 750,000 households had been won to the faith. Toda remained at the temple for a month, directing the various meetings and greeting the more than 210,000 pilgrims who came for the festivities. On April 1, fatigued but in jubilant spirits, he returned to Tokyo where he suddenly became ill and was taken to the hospital of Nihon University. Here on April 2, 1958, at the age of 58, Jōsei Toda died.

At Toda's funeral in the Aoyama Funeral Hall several hundred thousand people paid their respects, among whom were the Prime Minister, Nobusuke Kishi, and the Education Minister, Tō Matsunaga. At Taisekiji his tomb was erected beside the ancient pagoda, and the posthumous title of "Chief of all the preachers of the *Lotus Sūtra*" was bestowed upon him.

Growth of the Sōka Gakkai

Two years after Toda's death Sōka Gakkai claimed to have grown in membership from 800,000 family units to 1,300,000. By the end of 1961 the membership was reported in *The Mainichi Daily News* (July 4, 1962) as being 2.3 million. Sōka Gakkai, though registered locally, is not registered with the Education

Ministry and does not report its statistics officially. However, Tadakuni Nakaba, reporter for the *Asahi Shimbun* (in his book on Sōka Gakkai titled *Nihon no Chōryū,* Japan's Ebbing Tide, January 1968), reports the membership of Sōka Gakkai, as of March 31, 1967, to be 6,255,501 household units.

The "great march" of Sōka Gakkai which began with the proclamation of Toda in 1951 when he vowed that he would not be buried until 750,000 families had been won, is in evidence everywhere in Japan today. Not only in their regimental reviews where tens of thousands gather in the large stadiums of Yokohama or Ōsaka to watch the youth groups march in parade (over 100,000 attended the "Sōka Gakkai Olympics" staged in the wake of the 1964 Tokyo Olympic Games), or the political world where Sōka Gakkai candidates in ward, prefectural, metropolitan assembly, and National Diet elections have won signal victories, but also in the personal activities of individual members who "compass sea and land to make one proselyte," Sōka Gakkai poses a threat to the status quo of many segments of Japanese society.

The threat of Sōka Gakkai to Japanese political parties is treated in another chapter; suffice it to say here that the Socialist Party considered their success important enough to establish a study committee and publish a tract on Sōka Gakkai before the 1962 House of Councilors' election. Japan's all-powerful labor organization, Sōhyō (Japan Labor Union General Council), in 1957, after experiencing interference from Sōka Gakkai in the Coal Miners' Union affairs in Hokkaidō, established a "religious committee" which recommended counter measures to be taken against Sōka Gakkai at the general convention. In the religious world, Sōka Gakkai alone of the new religions is regarded as a threat to established Buddhism. At a meeting of the Kyōto Buddhist Council (November 8, 1961) sixty Buddhist leaders devoted their main attention to the challenge of Sōka Gakkai. The Butsuryū Denomination of Nichiren Buddhism organized an anti-Sōka Gakkai society. Higashi Honganji (the head temple of the Shin Buddhist Denomination) and the Sōtō Denomination of Zen have published tracts against Sōka Gakkai. The World Buddhism Association (Sekai Bukkyō Kyōkai), borrowing the term which has become identified with Sōka Gakkai proselytizing methods, *shakubuku*, published a book calling for a conversion of the Sōka Gakkai itself *(Sōka Gakkai o Shakubuku Suru)*. The Shingon Denomination of Buddhism published a book called *Kyōgen Sōka Gakkai o Sabaku* (Fanatic Sōka Gakkai on Trial), contending that Sōka Gakkai has distorted basic Buddhist teachings. Two refutations of Sōka Gakkai by Christian writers have appeared: *Sōka Gakkai no Machigai o Tadasu* (Correcting the Inaccuracies of Sōka Gakkai), and *Sōka Gakkai no Shakubuku ni Kotaeru* (An Answer to Sōka Gakkai's *Shakubuku*). Even other popular religions in Japan have become alarmed to such an extent that in the fall meeting, 1965, of the Union of New Religions in Japan an eight-point campaign against Sōka Gakkai and its political arm, the Kōmeitō, was launched because of its "threat to the freedom of worship guaranteed by the Constitution."

The organizational pyramid of Sōka Gakkai is at once complex and functional. The horizontal base is composed of "blocks" (borrowing the English word) which are subdivided into geographic areas. This horizontal structure is in turn integrated with a highly stratified vertical structure, expanding from top to bottom in the following manner: general headquarters (57 in number), headquarters (210), general areas (871), areas (3,806), districts (21,166), and squads (139,978). To indicate more specifically the membership in these different divisions, a squad, for example, is composed of from 50 to 550 family units, a district is made up of from 1,000 to 3,000 family units, and so forth. Leadership is provided by a president, at the head, and a Board of Directors consisting of 565 members, including a chairman and 43 vice-chairmen. Members of the board serve as heads of the various departments such as general business affairs, leadership, education, culture, finance, men, women, youth, students, high school, middle school, publications, public relations, and overseas affairs. In addition there are nineteen employed staff members. Running expenses amounting to over yen 2,600,000,000 a year are met in part by dues of yen 1,000 (about $2.78) collected four times a year from those who wish to be members of the finance committee, or what would commonly be called "supporters." In 1967 there were almost 400,000 such supporting members contributing approximately yen 1,600,000,000 (over $4 million). Hōjō, General Director of Sōka Gakkai, said that these finance committee members were selected men who could be called upon to donate a one-thousand yen bill any time it was needed. Proceeds from the sale of literature (twenty varieties) published by the Sōka Gakkai operated publishing house are said to total over a billion yen a year. Special thank offerings, of course, are frequently received by the temples of the faith, and especially by the head temple. On April 1, 1964, the Grand Reception Hall, a huge, modernistic ferro-concrete structure containing stones and building materials from forty-six countries, was dedicated at Taisekiji, the budget for which had been collected in a four-day fund-raising drive in July, 1961, in which members contributed almost $9 million. An even more magnificent building of marble, the Shō Hondō, which will house the sacred Worship Object, is scheduled for completion by 1970.

Youth activities are varied and are calculated to appeal to the young liberated generation. Sōka Gakkai offers strict physical training for the young men; up in the cold of the morning for long hikes and calisthenics—something that the student needs to prepare his body for the rigid demands of university life; pioneer trips into the frontier of Hokkaidō to plant trees, at the individual's own expense—something to demonstrate his desire to serve his fellow man, to connect him with nature, and to build up his country; mass chorus groups with stiff competition for admittance; "Lotus Sūtra Study Societies" on campuses such as Tokyo University; and, of course, political activity through campaigning for Sōka Gakkai candidates, which is a special drawing card to the modern youth in Japan who has not yet reached voting age, or to the voting youth who is looking for a place to make his vote "really count."

The Sōka Gakkai Student Department has a membership larger than that of Zengakuren (the student organization of the radical left). With a membership of 200,000, Sōka Gakkai's Student Department claims one out of every seven college students in Japan today. The Youth Department, with 3,847 squads for boys and 3,656 squads for girls, has a total membership of about four million.

Many converts are made from among the discontents and maladjusted in metropolitan areas. Great inroads have also been made into the coal mining districts of Kyūshū and Hokkaidō. It is reported that eighty percent of the miners in Yūbari Mine, Hokkaidō, are members of Sōka Gakkai.[6]

Now setting out on foreign conquest, Sōka Gakkai reported in January, 1968, some 150,000 overseas members. The first official mission was conducted in January and February of 1961, when the president and other leaders made an eighteen-day tour of Southeast Asia, "taking the true faith back to the land of its birth." By 1967 the president, Ikeda, had taken thirteen trips overseas visiting thirty or more countries.

World chapters of Sōka Gakkai now encircle the globe, including the United States, Germany, Paris (the European headquarters), Korea, Hong Kong, Rangoon, Bangkok, Saigon, Jakarta, Melbourne, Manila, Taipei, Okinawa; and in South America, Peru, Bolivia, Paraguay, Argentina, with headquarters in Brazil, where there are chapters in North São Paulo and West São Paulo. The goal is to establish overseas chapters in more than 70 foreign countries by 1970.

In 1965 the Nichiren Shō-shū Sōka Gakkai of America was officially registered as a religious body in the State of California. Under the leadership of Masayasu Sadanaga (Sokagakkai, Los Angeles Kaikan, 2102 East 1st St., Los Angeles 33, California) there are thirteen chapters in the United States: two in Los Angeles, Hollywood, San Diego, San Francisco, Sacramento, Seattle, Colorado, Chicago, Kentucky, St. Louis, New York, and Washington. The leader of the Riverside Group, San Bernadino District, with a membership of six families, is a non-Japanese American. The leader of the Young Men's Division, Hollywood District, testifies that "the practice of *shakubuku* [forcing others to convert] is like pouring more fuel into the fire of my life."

Over 1300 American delegates were flown in ten chartered flights to attend the celebrations in connection with the dedication of the Grand Reception Hall in April, 1964; and another nine chartered planes brought American pilgrims in the summer of 1967. In response to the show of dedication on the part of the American constituency, the president arranged for the purchase of ten acres of land in Etiwanda, California, to construct the first temple of the religion on American soil. The temple was dedicated on May 16, 1967. And in preparation for the future extension of the work on this continent, Sōka Gakkai created an English newspaper, *World Tribune,* the first issue being published in August, 1964. Said Ikeda, in a press interview, "In America we are not taking an anti-Christian position, but a non-Christian one."

Dissension and Disillusionment

Because of the tight nature of its organization it did not seem likely that sectionalism would gain much headway in Sōka Gakkai. The group continues to present a solid front, and there is no reason to doubt its basic unity, yet a small splinter faction has broken away from the main organization. The faction was organized by Masaki Sakura in 1960 under the name Kentoku Kai (Society to Make Virtue Apparent) and claimed fifty members upon its organization, though little has been heard of it since.

The leader of this faction claimed that many Sōka Gakkai members were becoming dissatisfied with their religion because of the tedious ritual requirement of two hours spent in worship each day.

It is futile to speculate on the number of losses through dissension and disillusionment suffered by the society. Doubtless the names of many who have withdrawn or become indifferent are not immediately (if ever) stricken from the rolls. But it is not uncommon to meet people who have dropped away after having been ardent followers for a year or two, and there are a few instances of public repudiation of faith in Sōka Gakkai.

A woman came crying to Sōka Gakkai headquarters in Tokyo one day in November, 1955.[7] Having worked day and night for the organization in an official capacity she had finally lost her husband and her children because they could not tolerate her fanaticism.

One man confessed that he had given in to the pressure put on him by a friend and joined the society. His business had not been doing well, and he thought that a new approach through religion might be of help, as his friend had promised. On the day on which he finally yielded, Sōka Gakkai members came to burn his gods. But things went from bad to worse. He continued, for a while, to attend the meetings and listened over and over again to the miraculous testimonies of what faith in the Worship Object had brought to others, but the testimonies rang untrue because he could see with his own eyes the ragged condition of the clothing of the children of these people. He couldn't believe that their faith had benefited them very much. When he took his troubles to the head of his squad, he reported, he met only rebuff and was reprimanded for lack of faith. Returning home he tore out the new Worship Object from his altar and ripped it to shreds. Eventually, he confessed to the reporter who told his story in the *Asahi Shinbun* (Asahi News, July 2, 1957), he was able to find success and happiness, but no thanks to Sōka Gakkai.

Another former convert who recanted gave his exclusive story to the reporter of the Buddhist magazine, *Daihōrin* (September, 1960). He claimed that he had known several who had quit the society. A woman factory worker under him who had been a squad leader finally gave up her faith. Another squad leader working under him came with complaints and criticism of Sōka Gakkai. This imprudence on the part of the under-worker before his boss, who at that time was still earnest about his faith, cost him his job.

The confessor told the reporter for the magazine that he himself began to doubt the sincerity of Sōka Gakkai because of the hypocrisy of so many leaders whom he had met. One district chief, he said, frankly revealed to him his own misgivings about the society, though in front of members he continued to reprove others for lack of faith. Another disillusionment came when he visited the head temple. He was shocked to see Toda come to the lecture inebriated.

After the former convert finally made his decision to withdraw from Sōka Gakkai he was visited by twelve or more from the student department and threatened, but he realized no ill effects from these intimidations. In fact, his business had improved after he left the society. He now has confidence in his own ability without dependence upon any magical assistance from the Worship Object. His decision to withdraw, he confessed, was precipitated by the fact that his faith in the teachings of Sōka Gakkai had caused friction with his mother and father, who were members of a Zen denomination. Furthermore, he could not face the ridicule of colleagues in his business outlets throughout the country who made fun of Sōka Gakkai and the members of the society. To top it all, he said, he did not feel like a true Japanese in times of village and religious festivals because, as a follower of the Nichiren Shō Denomination, he was not permitted to participate. Having withdrawn from the society he is free again to take part in traditional Japanese religious celebrations though he still maintains a deep respect for Nichiren "as a buddha." He mailed back his Worship Object to the headquarters in hopes that his name would be removed from the membership list.

A census taken by the United Church of Christ in Japan in the year 1960 corroborates much of what this disillusioned convert reported.[8] The census was conducted among 200 Christian churches, carefully selected from fourteen areas including the four major islands and the chief metropolitan centers, urban, suburban, and rural areas. Converts to Christianity from non-Christian religions were asked, among other questions, why they had previously belonged to the non-Christian religion and the reason for which they finally left this religion to convert to Christianity.

It is interesting to note that the survey revealed that the greatest number of converts to religious sects such as Sōka Gakkai claimed to have been attracted through the personality of some member of the group—either the leader or a layman. Of course, desire for some particular temporal benefit was also listed as a major attraction. But it is worthy of note that the people questioned were in turn repelled by the very agents to whom they had formerly been attracted. The answer, of course, is that what they had thought to be true in the beginning concerning the faith and personality of members later appeared to them to have been illusion or hypocrisy.

Present Leadership of Sōka Gakkai

The phenomenal success of Sōka Gakkai in winning converts is due in large measure to the ability of the society's leaders. It is doubtful whether the organization will be able to produce another leader like Toda, but in an organization as large as this it is not surprising to find lesser leaders capable of continuing the operation of the machinery that is running under the impetus of the original inspiration.

Yoshihei Kodaira is one of these men. Kodaira has remained in the background so far as the general public is concerned, but he is the man most responsible for the promulgation of the powerful propaganda literature: the *Daibyaku Renge* (Great White Lotus) and *Daisan Bunmei* (Great Third Civilization), monthly magazines; the *Ushio* (Tide), a magazine aimed at youth and sold at newsstands; the *Seikyō Gurafu* (The Seikyō Graphic), a pictorial; the *Seikyō Shinbun* (The Seikyō News, in the Japanese language), a daily newspaper with a circulation of three million in 1967; and a number of books for the indoctrination of members. Head of the education department of Sōka Gakkai, Kodaira has been an employee of the Labor Ministry and was elected from the national constituency (with five other Sōka Gakkai candidates) to the Upper House (House of Councilors) in 1959.

Another indispensable cog in the wheel is Hiroshi Hōjō (age 45), political boss of the group, who was elected to the Upper House in both 1956 and 1962. Chairman of the Board of Directors of Sōka Gakkai and head of the culture department, he is considered second only to the president. Member of the seventy-third graduating class of the military academy, he is a hard, disciplined rightist. Through his influence a large number of fellow graduates of the military academy have been brought into the organization. He is top man in organization and politics.

On April 9, 1960, upon the nomination of Chairman Koizumi, the Board of Directors appointed Daisaku Ikeda (then 32 years of age) to serve as the third president of Sōka Gakkai. (Though accepting the title of *kaichō,* which means "president" or "chairman," Ikeda asks members not to refer to him as *Sensei,* which means "teacher," but to reserve this title for Makiguchi and Toda.) Born January 2, 1928, the fifth son in the home of a seaweed merchant in Ōmori, Tokyo, whose business was virtually destroyed by the bombing in World War II, Ikeda was forced to go to work at an early age to help support his family. For a time he worked in the Niigata Iron Works where he met Kaneko, daughter of the vice-chairman of Sōka Gakkai's Board of Directors. The two were married when he was 23 and she 19 years of age. Today they have three sons, ages 14, 12, and 9.

Ikeda had served under Toda from the time he was 19, being appointed as a member of the executive group of the youth department when it was formed in 1951. He soon was promoted to the rank of chief of staff, working directly under Toda. In this capacity he was responsible for carrying out the more aggressive policies and actions of the youth department. But Ikeda's chief talent seemed to lie in the political realm. He was soon made responsible for Sōka Gakkai election campaigns, while serving, at the same time, as chairman of the publicity department of Sōka Gakkai headquarters. After the death of Toda, Ikeda served as chairman of the general affairs department until he was chosen to be the third president. Though he does not possess the charismatic qualities of Toda, still he is able to harangue an audience of 100,000 in a voice so much like the master's that the two are easily confused when listened to from a recording. He, too, is a student of the *Lotus Sūtra*, as Toda was, and his lectures, called *Lectures on Buddhism,* have been published in English by the society.

In an interview he described a typical work day. Usually he makes his appearance at the Shinanomachi headquarters at ten. His plush office is seldom occupied, for Ikeda is in constant conferences and work sessions with staff members. He is paid a monthly salary of yen 200,000 (about $555) as managing editor of the Seikyō Press. Many of his working hours are spent in looking over copy from publications of the various branches of Sōka Gakkai related organizations: the Kōmeitō (political arm), Tōyō Gakujitsu Kenkyū-jo (an institute located in Tokyo University), Ajia Bunka Kyōkai (Asia Culture Association), Ushio Shuppansha (The Ushio Publishing House), Dainichi Rengesha (The Dainichi Renge Publishing House), and Min-on (The Folk Music Association). Royalties from his own books, *Risshō Ankokuron* (a commentary on a writing by Nichiren of the same name), *Hoke Shuyō-shō* (Guide to the *Lotus Sūtra*), *Ningen Kakumei* (English translation: *The Human Revolution*) which is a sequel to Toda's autobiography under the same name, *Bunka to Shūkyō* (Culture and Religion), *Seiji to Shūkyō* (Politics and Religion), and *Kagaku to Shūkyō* (Science and Religion), this last heading the national best-seller list in 1965, all bring in an additional yen 6 million (approximately $17,000). These royalties, however, he added, are allocated to meet expenses of Sōka Gakkai's political party, travel abroad, and to help provide an insurance fund for members of the staff.

During the day Ikeda reads as many newspapers and periodicals as he can, remembering his teacher's injunction, "A man without a social conscience does not become a leader." At lunchtime he brought out a lunch his wife had packed for him. Though his blue suit was custom-made, from imported goods, the Ikeda family live simply, without ostentation, in a small residence in Ōta Ward, Tokyo. He commuted by train to his office until believers of the society began to show such deference to him in public that he became embarrassed before fellow commuters. He then changed to a Cedric (Japan's luxury limousine), and recently moved nearer the headquarters. His one luxury, he confessed, is an hour in the barber chair twice each month. He is clean-cut, neat, immaculate in dress, and extremely courteous in speech— quite the reverse image from his predecessor, Toda. He has the appearance of a young, successful businessman, and his selection at this time in the history of Sōka Gakkai marks a decisive shift in direction. Some interpret this to mean that the youth organization of Sōka Gakkai has taken the reins. N. H. K. Radio commentator Hiroi Takase calls it the victory of the Toda disciples over the old-school Makiguchi disciples.[9]

At his inauguration on May 3, 1960, in the spacious Great Auditorium of Nihon University, Tokyo, before an audience of over 20,000 followers, Ikeda spoke as follows:

> I am young, but from today, representing Toda's disciples, with the goal of disseminating the way of salvation laid down by the Buddha, I take the leadership for the march ahead. . . . Sōka Gakkai is the greatest ally of the people. The enemy to man is false religion. ('False religion casts the people into hell;

the Upright Dharma makes of them Buddha.') Such is the
golden saying of the Great Holy One, Nichiren, but he who
preached exactly in accordance to this golden saying was none
other than our beloved *Sensei,* Jōsei Toda. Taking up his
banner, let us his followers pursue after the extermination of
all false religion.[10]

We will now take a look at some of the implications of this
campaign to "exterminate all false religion."

Nenbutsu mugen,
zen tenma,
shingon bōkoku,
ritsu kokuzoku

The Nenbutsu is hell;
Zen is a devil;
Shingon is the nation's ruin;
and Ritsu is a traitor to the country.

(from *Risshō Ankokuron,* by Nichiren)

五章

THE SMASHING OF IDOLS

The most controversial characteristics of Sōka Gakkai have been its iconoclastic attitude and its fanatical conversion technique. In order to save mankind in this age "when the true Buddhist Dharma has been forgotten," it has launched an aggressive campaign to eradicate all vestiges of "false religions." This campaign has involved forced conversions and a systematic destruction of all their icons, that is, all religious symbols formerly used by its converts.

On the night of April 28, 1952, a group of young men formed a long queue in front of the Main Hall of Taisekiji. With bamboo flutes, drums, and a banner reading "The Evil Priest Who Killed Makiguchi *Sensei*," they marched up the stone steps, seized a priest by the name of Ogasawara, and took him off to an inner room where they held a Kangaroo Court. Impetuous Sōka Gakkai youth had beseiged the inner courts of their own religion in righteous indignation for what had happened to their founder during the war.

During the Second World War this priest allegedly had compromised with the military leaders and advised Sōka Gakkai followers to receive without opposition the talisman from the Ise Shrine. (It was because of his refusal to accept this talisman that the revered founder, Makiguchi, and others in Sōka Gakkai were imprisoned, charged with the crime of *lèse majesté*; and it was in prison that Makiguchi died.) Moreover, the priest had compounded his crime by asserting that the Shintō kami were "the basic reality" and the buddhas only "a reflection," thereby being guilty of assigning the Buddha to an inferior position to the Shintō kami.[1] Consequently, beaming a flashlight in the old man's face, the youths demanded: "Were you right when you said that the kami are 'the basic reality' and the buddhas are only 'a reflection'? Is the Great Worship Object only 'a reflection'?" Trembling and stammering, if we are to believe the report, the old priest answered: "I was mistaken. What I said was wrong. It was bad. Praise be the *Lotus Sūtra. Namu Myōhōrengekyō, Namu Myōhōrengekyō.*"

This incident, which later became known as the Badger *(tanuki)* Incident in the annals of Sōka Gakkai, gave the organization such a reputation for violence that a religious council of the Nichiren Shō Denomination was called. It was decided (1) that the young men should apologize through the heads of their local temples, (2) that Jōsei Toda, who was held responsible for the incident, should be dismissed, and (3) that he should never again be permitted to worship at the head temple. However, the issue was settled by Toda going to Taisekiji and apologizing to the temple authorities for the deed.

Though Sōka Gakkai leaders are not happy with the image which overardent followers have created, the fact remains that the general public has come to look upon Sōka Gakkai followers as a group of "violent religious fanatics."[2]

Nichiren's Condemnation of Other Faiths

From its beginning Nichiren Buddhism has been noted for its idol smashing. With the founder, Nichiren, this took the form of invectives against contemporary religions—chiefly faith in Amida Buddha and Pure Land Buddhism—and memorials against the government, which, he claimed, was inviting foreign invasion and the nation's ruin by countenancing false teachings. During the intervening centuries most of Nichiren's followers gradually outgrew his fanaticism (which is inconsistent with traditional Buddhism's teaching of the "middle way"), but the radical spirit of the founder was preserved in the Nichiren Shō Denomination and a few other small groups. Its more crass manifestations are rarely seen today in Japan except in Sōka Gakkai.

Of Shintō, Nichiren claimed, in the *Risshō Ankokuron,* that the good deities (kami) of Shintō had left the country and only the evil ones remained. Therefore, he concluded, "calamities and sorrows" had befallen the nation. In 1264 he was on his way to the execution ground where he was to be beheaded for his crime of *lèse majesté* against the Regent Tokimune; he had publicly declared that the regent was destined for hell. As the execution party paused for rest in the vicinity of the Tsurugaoka Hachiman Shintō Shrine in Kamakura, Nichiren challenged the kami to come to his rescue. His prayer was more an act of defiance than an entreaty. Nichiren did not openly deny the existence of the kami, but he had little use for them.

Nichiren regarded himself as the prophet of "true Buddhism," which he claimed had been replaced throughout the land by false religions, that is, false Buddhism. "It is said in the *Sūtra of the Great Decease (Nirvāna Sūtra),*" he wrote, "that if a monk sees a man injuring Buddhism and fails to reprove him, he is a worthless brother; but if he speaks up and reproves him, he is a true brother. I am scarcely worthy to be called a monk, yet I am trying to do my duty."[3]

The calamities which had recently shaken the country were a punishment visited upon the nation for its apostasy, according to Nichiren:

> Because of pestilence and disaster many are turning to religion. "A sharp sword is the Name of Mida," some say and turn in prayer to the Lord of the Western Land, whilst others take up the magic charms and formulae against disease, which belong to the Lord of the Eastern Quarter. . . . When I come to examine things more closely in the light of the Scriptures, I find that the whole world is in rebellion against what is right, and that men have universally become the slaves of evil; further, that on account of this not only have the good deities left the country, but even the saints abandon the place and refuse to come back to it. Evil spirits and demons have come to take their places, and calamities and sorrows have befallen us.[4]

To Tendai Buddhism alone Nichiren showed some deference. He held a deep respect for the wisdom of Tendai Daishi, the Chinese priest who founded the Tendai school of Buddhism; but he declared that the original teaching of the master had been perverted by Jikaku (died A.D. 864) and his followers, whom he accused of "slandering the Dharma."

According to Nichiren, Tendai Daishi's teaching was efficacious for the period of the "Accommodated Dharma" (beginning one thousand years after Gautama's death and extending for a thousand years), but it was useless for men living in the period of the "End of the Dharma" (which Nichiren believed his own incarnation in A.D. 1222 to have inaugurated):

> . . . even if the identical truth revealed by Tendai Daishi and Dengyō Daishi remained, it would be like last year's calendar in the present time of the End of the Dharma.[5]

Though his criticism of Tendai Buddhism was mild, Nichiren nonetheless declared that the Tendai Denomination had become corrupt and that the teachings of the founder were no longer relevant or efficacious to man.

Nichiren's strongest reproof was directed at Hōnen (1133–1212), the founder of Amida Buddhism in Japan (but why he was silent with reference to Shinran, immediate disciple of Hōnen, remains a mystery). The popularity of the so-called Amida Sects (*Jōdo* and *Jōdo Shin-shū,* Pure Land Buddhism) had caused the other temples of the country to fall into ruins and their priests to starve, according to Nichiren. In choleric idiom Hōnen is denounced, in the writings of Nichiren, as a "deceiver" and a "blasphemer."

Shingon Buddhism (an esoteric faith) was attacked for its sin of "dissecting the body of Buddha." Like the Kegon Denomination, it had elevated the Buddha Dainichi (Mahāvairochana) to the head of the Buddhist pantheon, worshiping him as the "Body of Essence." In Shingon the Buddha Amida is said to possess the "Body of Bliss" and the historical Buddha (Gautama) the "Body of Manifestation." Because they had denied his material body, wrote Nichiren, the followers of Shingon were like a prince who despised his father, the king, as of no rank,[6] a most damning statement in a class-conscious society. Shingon, he declared, relied upon *sūtras* that were accommodated teachings (the *Dainichi-kyō, Kongōchō-kyō,* and *Soshitsuchi-kyō*) and which, he said, have no relation to man in the period of the "End of the Dharma." He claimed that the most evil teaching of Shingon was its censorship and ridicule of the historical Buddha, Gautama, whom it had replaced by a buddha (Dainichi) considered by Nichiren to be so ethereal as to have no immanent relationship to man at all. Though Nichiren recognized the existence of Dainichi, he considered this Buddha concept to be an accommodation (*hōben*) given by Gautama for the purpose of instructing his disciples. Moreover, Nichiren criticized Shingon for stealing and distorting Tendai Daishi's teaching of the *ichinensanzen.*

The Nara group—Kusha, Jōjitsu, and Ritsu—were also condemned for dissecting the body of the Buddha. Through their worship of the Buddha, Gautama, the "Body of Manifestation," these Buddhist denominations were guilty of bringing the Buddha down to a low plane, as if a prince should consider himself to be the son of a person of low rank. Nichiren denounced the Sanron and Hossō denominations for worshiping only the "Body of Bliss," and said that they were like a prince who considered his father to be of the rank of a samurai (a high rank in feudal society but not the highest). He asserted that in all of these groups the believers, like a child who could not recognize the true value of his father, failed to recognize the true nature of the Buddha. In the *Lotus Sūtra,* taught Nichiren, the inadequacy of these partial views of the Buddha is exposed because of the final teaching of the unity of the three bodies of the Buddha as one.

Zen, with its faith in self-effort (*jiriki*) and its worship of the historical Gautama himself as the "Body of Manifestation," according to Nichiren, debases the *Lotus Sūtra* as inconsequential. Nichiren, who considered the *Lotus Sūtra* to be the highest revelation of the Dharma, could not tolerate such sacrilege. The Zen practice of meditation, *zazen,* and the continual searching of the mind for truth elicit from Nichiren the caustic criticism:

> Pray that you may be the instructor of your mind and not instructed by your mind.[7]

Zen, too, is condemned as a "slanderer of the Dharma" and the handiwork of the devil.

In recapitulation Nichiren summed up his contempt for all other Buddhist denominations with one sweeping invective: "The

Nenbutsu [referring to Amida Buddhism] is hell; Zen is a devil; Shingon is the nation's ruin; and Ritsu is a traitor to the country."

Sōka Gakkai's Campaign Against "False Religion"

The torch of witch hunting was taken up very effectively by Sōka Gakkai; to members of the society, all religions, except Nichiren Shō, are "false religion." The extermination of false beliefs—which misguided the people, plunged the nation into despair, and ultimately brought about the country's defeat in World War II—is the battle cry of Sōka Gakkai members as it was of Nichiren himself.

The Shintō kami are ridiculed. Money offerings must be presented to them; but what use, they ask, has a kami for money? Paper talismen are supposed to provide protection from all manner of misfortune—fire, theft, sickness—and to guarantee peace in the home and success in business; but in six months or a year the holder is supposed to burn his talisman and secure a new one! If there were any power in these scraps of paper, Sōka Gakkai believers declare, no one would ever think of burning them. Finally, they argue that if a person is in need he usually goes to the place where he can satisfy his need. If he requires healing, he goes to a doctor; if he wants fish, he goes to the fishmonger. Praying at a Shintō shrine for healing, says Sōka Gakkai, is like praying to a fishmonger. Various superstitions (e.g., if three persons have their picture taken together, the one in the middle will meet an early death) are ridiculed.

Ancestral gods (or kami), belief in which constitutes the core of the Shintō religion, are not denied peremptorily. The Sōka Gakkai follower may render thanks to his ancestors but not worship.[8] The numerous kami of Shinto are included among the deva gods of Buddhism and then made sport of, much in the manner that Nichiren treated them. Without denying them outright, Sōka Gakkai claims that the good kami have left Japan and that only the evil kami remain.

In the *Shakubuku Kyōten* (Manual on Forced Conversions) the origin of Shintō in animism is briefly traced and criticized as having no doctrine at all. The existence of the Sun Goddess,

Amaterasu (the imperial ancestress), is not refuted, but it is contended that she too, like the other good kami, has left Japan and will not return until the entire nation has turned to the true religion, the Nichiren Shō Denomination. Buddhism, according to Sōka Gakkai, had already cut itself off from its true roots by the time Nichiren appeared. Sōka Gakkai accuses Buddhism of vacillation and compromise in its endeavor always to stay in the good graces of the governing powers. Thus, they say, Buddhism was indolent and oblivious of the needs of the people in the Edo period (1600–1868) and allowed itself to be used as a tool of the government against Christianity. In the Meiji era (1868–1912) it joined the group in power and then catered to the military during their rise to power in the Shōwa period (1926–   ). Today, in the postwar age, Buddhism parades itself as democratic!

To Sōka Gakkai all forms of Buddhism, other than its own, are dry bones with no meat of doctrine, no power of the Dharma, no Buddha dynamism. As for the priests, they are priest in name only, barren of faith and practice. The Buddhist priest's only concern is to eke out a living through performance of funeral and memorial rites for the dead, and watch-care of the graves.

Some of the popular faiths which are somewhat obscurely connected to Nichiren Buddhism are the Reiyū Kai, Risshō Kōsei Kai, Kōdō Kyōdan, Kokuchū Kai, Nihonzan Myōhōji, and Dai jō-kyō. These new religions are criticized for their practices of ancestor worship, onomancy, shallow social works, copying of the sacred inscription, and so forth.

In the *Shakubuku Kyōten,* Sōka Gakkai suggests several reasons which are thought to contribute to the success of Tenrikyō, a leading rival. Among the reasons listed are (1) the general ignorance of the people regarding religion, (2) a large, impressive headquarters establishment, (3) an attractive program for down-and-out people, (4) the offer of simple guidance for daily life, (5) the practice of healing, (6) the training of the followers not to think of misfortune as misfortune. The most cutting criticism which Sōka Gakkai makes of Tenrikyō, however, is that the believers are poor and that their religion, far from helping them to improve their lot, encourages personal bankruptcy for the benefit of the headquarters.

The teaching found in the scriptures of Konkōkyō is criticized by Sōka Gakkai as being nothing but common-sense ethics. The worship is despised as consisting of the basest kind of religious practice. From the point of view of Sōka Gakkai, Konkōkyō's teaching that man will be redeemed if he can rid himself of all desire is ridiculous, since a man with no human desires would have no reason to go on living. (The complete secularization of Buddhism in the teaching of Sōka Gakkai is in evidence in this criticism.) Presented as conclusive proof that Konkōkyō is indeed a "false religion" is the incidence of the destruction by fire of the headquarters in 1925.

Seichō no Ie is labeled as a "business concern" or publishing house rather than a religion in the criticism of Sōka Gakkai. People are promised salvation if they will carry a book in their pockets. They do not grapple with the problem of the origin of unhappiness and sickness, but simply deny the existence of such things. They mistakenly try to synthesize Christianity and Buddhism, which are poles apart. They deny matter, claiming that everything is in the mind. A person is told to be grateful for everything. Even if he gets his foot trampled on in a crowded streetcar, the believer is supposed to say to the unthoughtful person who trod on him, "I am so grateful you didn't get your shoe dirty." This kind of teaching is said to be modeled on Christianity's impractical teaching of "love thine enemy."

Christianity is the universal non-Buddhist religion singled out for attack. The Christian idea of a Creator-God is considered to be an anachronism and unscientific. The existence of the self or soul is denied. Christianity is called a religion without power to change man's present condition. It is said to be inferior to Buddhism. While Buddhism promises salvation to all, Christianity threatens the unbeliever with eternal damnation. The doctrines of the divinity and the resurrection of Christ are outside the province of rational thought. Because it has no teaching concerning the three worlds (referring to the theory of reincarnation), Christianity is incomplete. Buddhism alone grapples with the main problems of life: the origin and the goal of suffering. Belief in a heaven to which one goes after death is, like that of the Pure Land of the Amida sects, nothing but a fabrication. Christians are schizophrenic; in talking of God, love, goodness, sin, the followers of Christianity are frantically searching for something which, if they only knew it, can be found in the Worship Object of the Nichiren Shō faith. Trying to cover up the impotence of their own faith, Christians lose themselves in social works by which they lead others astray.

How, they ask, does Christianity regard the following contradictions:

(1) The contradiction involved in saying that only believers will be saved, yet that there is obligation to save those who have gone astray.

(2) The fact that it was the same Christian Church which preached "love thine enemies," that persecuted Galileo and other scientists.

(3) The dropping of the atomic bomb directly on the Japanese Christian town of Nagasaki.

(4) While the Great Holy One was victorious when the suffering of Tatsunokuchi threatened his life, Christ suffered a miserable, violent death.

(5) Not one of Christ's prophecies was fulfilled.

(6) Isn't the fact that internal disunity, which is apparent through the proposed ecumenical movement, proof that its doctrine is impotent?

(7) While speaking of the poor in spirit and the pure in heart the Vatican has had a history of colossal power and political pressure.

(8) Since the various sects contain false doctrine and teach principles that cast men deeper into sin, turning their backs on Christ, which of all the Christian sects is the true tradition and doctrine?[9]

Forced Conversion

Three terms in the Buddhist or, more specifically, the Nichiren Buddhist tradition are important for an understanding of this faith: *Shōju, shakubuku,* and *hōbōbarai.* The latter two provide the rationale for Sōka Gakkai's frenetic proselytizing activities and its intolerance of all other religious faiths, even including other branches of its own faith.

Shakubuku literally means "to destroy and conquer." It is an old term which originally was used by Nichiren to designate the conversion activity of his followers, but it had long since been outgrown and generally forgotten even by most Nichiren denominations until its revival by Sōka Gakkai. Today there is hardly an adult Japanese who does not know the word. The term occurred originally in the *Shōmangyō* (The Sūtra of the Earnest Resolve), in connection with a parallel term, *shōju,* which means literally "acceptance." *Shakubuku* designates intolerant propaganda and pressure to produce a forced conversion; *shōju* is a tolerant approach by means of moral suasion. Nichiren stressed that tolerant, moral suasion could be used with some men, but that with others it was necessary to use intolerant methods.

Examples of the use of moral suasion are numerous, but these are seldom sensational enough to make news.

A woman follower of Sōka Gakkai, without any thought of financial remuneration, served as practical nurse and housemaid for three years in the home of a neighbor who was dying of cancer. Inevitably, then—so the story goes—when the patient finally died her husband and all the members of the family of the deceased became converts.

A tenement dweller felt perfectly free to call upon her Sōka Gakkai neighbor for help in the middle of the night when her father was being rushed to the hospital with stomach pains. Later, after this man had died of stomach cancer, the same neighbor stayed away from her work for three days (sacrificing badly needed wages) in order to help the family with funeral arrangements. Here, too, a conversion followed.

Twenty of the thirty residents in a dormitory for working girls in Yokohama recently joined Sōka Gakkai after one of the girls was healed of scars of the atomic bomb on her face. The healing "miracle" was accomplished by a plastic surgeon through accepted medical means, but it was a devout Sōka Gakkai member who insisted that she could be healed, and it was this believer who worked and prayed until the "miracle" was accomplished.

It is stories of *shakubuku,* however, which have mainly reached the attention of the press, and it is these which are responsible for the generally unfavorable public attitude toward Sōka Gakkai. *Shakubuku* often employs a technique of intimidation carried out in a very systematic manner. Two or three members will approach a prospect at his place of business in the presence of customers, or in his home in front of guests, and will not relent until the object of their attack has promised to become a member. An ordinary housewife is often subjected to conversion efforts from a delivery man, the gas meter man, or even from former classmates and school friends who ostensibly just drop in for a chat.

The reason for this frenzied conversion activity is not difficult to understand. President Ikeda, speaking to a group of Sōka Gakkai leaders in Nakano Ward, Tokyo (June 17, 1960), pointed out three reasons for *shakubuku* activity: (1) It is the quickest route to achieving buddhahood and happiness in this life; (2) it is necessary in order to break the chain of karma and cut oneself loose from the effects of deeds of one's past existence; (3) through winning another by means of *shakubuku* the believer shares his happiness and reaps additional merit for himself. According to Ikeda, this is "killing three birds with one stone."

Consequently members compete to see who can win the most converts and thus acquire greater merit. At first a member may approach a friend or an acquaintance who has indicated in some way that he may be undergoing some particular trial or misfortune—usually business difficulties or sickness. If the person does not turn the Sōka Gakkai caller away absolutely, other members will hear about it, and an onslaught will begin from all quarters. Whenever a person seems likely to give in, members begin coming in teams; but a new convert is credited only to the person who can show that he won him, and the membership is registered in this member's own group wherever that may be. Those with a large number of successes to their credit are rewarded with positions as the head of troops, districts, and so forth.

Toda, however, was aware of the danger of fanaticism and often cautioned against irrational behavior. In an essay titled "The Middle Path" (June 1, 1954), he appealed to his followers to be sensible in their religious fervor:

> The attitude of the man of faith is the attitude of the Middle Path. Of course there is merit in *shakubuku;* and, if a man has something special to ask for, *shakubuku* is extremely important. But there are some of you who are neglecting your work to do *shakubuku,* and then weeping because the money doesn't come in. This is ridiculous. Business is business. Do your business and dedicate your free time to *shakubuku.* The man who hears about *shakubuku* and shoves his work aside to engage in *shakubuku* alone is off his rocker. Business is business, and it takes planning and thought. The basic power which enables a man to plan and think is the power of faith. That which enables a man to cut down his losses and increase his gains is the Wonderful Reason of faith—the power of faith. . . .[10]

Moreover, in what purports to be a definitive history of the faith and doctrine of Nichiren Shō and Sōka Gakkai, a book put out by the Lotus Sūtra Society (a Sōka Gakkai organization of students of Tokyo University), the section on *shakubuku* is illuminating in its attempt to make this activity more acceptable to society:

> A person hears about the Nichiren Shō Denomination or Sōka Gakkai from a member of Sōka Gakkai. This is *shakubuku.* Since there are members in every class and branch of society people hear about it through their relations with friends, acquaintances, social companions, neighbors, relatives, and so on. As for the place where *shakubuku* activity is conducted, it varies from the occasion of receiving a visitor into one's home, or visiting in another's home, after work, on a trip, or at a discussion meeting of Sōka Gakkai.
>
> Opposition and criticism may accompany *shakubuku. Shakubuku* is often referred to as "forcing faith," or as a "violation of privacy," but is it indeed so? Can a person be forced to believe? . . . *shakubuku* first and last takes the attitude of charity (*jihi*). It is "an invitation to true faith," coming from a desire to eliminate mistaken religions which are the root of unhappiness and to make another happy. It is pure, sincere

activity based upon "conviction" which has back of it abundant experience. But there are a great many people who are opposed to *shakubuku* either because of ignorance or because of [its insistence on] discarding traditional religions which have become a habit. There are people who have a negative psychological reaction to the very word *jashūkyō* (false religions).[11]

Finally, President Ikeda has also appealed to members to "speak and act with common sense." He has reprimanded them for making obscene gestures when passing before Shintō shrines and temples of other denominations and calling out in loud voices, *"Jashū!"* ("False religions!") And he has forbidden *shakubuku* activity on the job and frowned upon the practice of staying at a neighbor's house until the early morning hours trying to win a convert.

In spite of these admonitions, however, the practice of trying to force people to convert has continued throughout the years, although admittedly there has been a gradual diminution in reports of extreme violence.

To give an early example of what has happened, the unprecedented increase in members throughout the mining community of Yūbari created quite a sensation in 1957, when a clash with the coal miners' union turned the nation's attention to that area. It was reported in the *Shūkan Asahi* (Asahi Weekly), July 7, 1957, that Sōka Gakkai members would call on the housewife in her husband's absence and threaten her, saying, "We hope your husband comes home safely from work today," or "It will be fortunate indeed if your child develops normally."

Intimidation of the parents of middle school children by schoolteachers doing home visitation were reported in Hyōgo Prefecture, and a headline of the *Yomiuri Shinbun* (Yomiuri News), July 6, 1957, read, "Sōka Gakkai Becomes Problem in Tokyo." This article told how schoolteachers in Tokyo elementary schools used the regular home visitation program as an opportunity to proselytize. Parents were told that if they did not become members of Sōka Gakkai their children would become abnormal. When the matter was investigated by the education committee of local school districts, one teacher defended herself by saying that, since she had gained so much happiness from her faith, she felt it was only natural to try to offer to help when she visited an evidently unhappy home.

A still earlier case of forced conversion, which is typical of many others, was reported in the *Shin Shūkyō Shinbun* (New Religions News), November 20, 1955. Because she did not say "no" firmly enough to discourage them, three or four young members called on a young woman for several days in succession, each time warning her that if she did not become a believer within a week some terrible calamity would befall her home. On the last day they said they wouldn't move until she gave in, and she finally allowed them to sign her name at two o'clock in the morning.

A more recent example is the experience of the Reverend Mitsuzō Gotō, a Christian minister and Professor of Evangelism at Japan Christian College, who tells of being lured into a Sōka Gakkai meeting in July, 1963, where he was given the third degree for several hours. A veteran with thirty years of pastoral experience, Mr. Gotō reportedly turned the tables on his attackers, answering every criticism which they made of Christianity, taking the young members to task for screaming at him without giving him a chance to explain his position, and, in the end, bringing his antagonists to the point where they begged to be released so that they could go home to get some sleep. A similar attempt at conversion of Christians occurred the previous year in Okinawa. When members began to gather for an evening meeting in the Kin Baptist Church, a group of Sōka Gakkai youth suddenly appeared and forced some of the Christians to accompany them to their own discussion meeting in a building not far away.

The following incidents have been reported in the news in recent years:

Feb. 10, 1962, *Asahi Shinbun:* Sixty-eight Sōka Gakkai youth with saws and pliers entered a Buddhist cemetery at midnight on February 10, broke down barricades set up by the Buddhist Association of the village, and routed the policemen in order to conduct a burial for the father of one Wakameda Kushiro (age 45) in Karasuyama, Tochigi Prefecture. Priest Iso of the Ichijūin Temple of the Shingon Denomination told the police

that Kushiro had been refused burial rights at the cemetery
since his lease on the family plot had expired and since seven
years before he had joined Sōka Gakkai and withdrawn from
the denomination which owned the burial ground.

April 23, 1962, *Asahi Shinbun:* Mrs. Sui Tamura (age 56) was
beaten over the head and bruised about the face by her son
in the latter's fanatic effort to destroy the family Buddhist
altar and convert his mother to faith in Sōka Gakkai. Fleeing
her son and daughter-in-law the mother sought asylum at the
local police station at 11:00 p.m., on April 21. The incident
took place in a village called Seiro in Niigata Prefecture.

October 27, 1964, *Asahi Shinbun:* Tadashi Fujiwara (age 33)
was arrested on a murder charge after being apprehended at
an inn in Okayama where he had been staying for several
days. Himself a Sōka Gakkai member, it is reported that he
became angry at the incessant noise created by two Sōka
Gakkai men in an adjoining room and attacked them with a
butcher knife. Another Sōka Gakkai man entered the fight,
and Fujiwara injured all three of them seriously, one of them
dying later in the hospital.

December 11, 1964, *Nagasaki Shinbun:* Momosuke Maeda, of
Sasebo, registered a complaint against Sōka Gakkai members
of the 99th District for their excessive intimidation of his
daughter (age 19) who had just got out of the sickbed. It
appears that first she had been persuaded by two school friends
to attend a meeting where she was the target of browbeating
by eleven members at once and told that if she did not convert
she would never find happiness, but if she converted she was
certain to pass the examination at the beautician school for a
national license. When she refused, her signature stamp was
affixed to an application for membership against her will.

March 19, 1965, *Ōsaka Shin Yūkan:* In Tottori an injunction
was issued against a nurse in the local hospital on the charge
that in her fanatical attempt to convert a patient she had
neglected to report his physical condition to the doctor in time
to save him from dying.

March 30, 1965, *Hokkaidō Shinbun:* A youth, Teruo Suzuki
(age 23), who was employed in a factory for the manufacture
of automobile interiors, in Obihiro, was arrested by the police
on the charge of arson. Upon his own confession it appears
that he had set fire to the house of a party whom he had tried

to convert to Sōka Gakkai but had failed. In his effort to convert the prospect he is said to have threatened, "If you don't convert your house will catch fire."

It is interesting to see that effort is being made to mitigate the effect of such publicity on would-be converts. For foreign readers of Sōka Gakkai English publications, the term *shakubuku* itself is redefined to help the image:

> *Shakubuku* means to introduce the teachings of Nichiren Daishonin to non-believers by relating the divine benefits of faith. It aims at achieving people's happiness, a prosperous society and world peace. . . . Disregarding its different shades of meaning, people have interpreted *Shakubuku* as something like "break and subdue." Thus, they have misjudged the Sokagakkai's propagation activities as coercive or even violent. Such a misunderstanding is quite ridiculous.[11]

However, conversion through these high-pressure methods oftentimes is extremely superficial. Though an individual sometimes joins to put a stop to the nagging of a friend, he may try to withdraw the commitment when the pressure is off. But superstition and fear of divine punishment are employed to keep a new member from falling away.

Hōbōbarai means, literally, "sweeping out all the slanderers of the Dharma." To "slander the Dharma" is to commit the unpardonable sin of Buddhism. Specifically *hōbōbarai* means to remove, forcibly or otherwise, the talisman and amulets connected with the worship of Shintō kami and to destroy statues and icons of any alien faith.

In Fukushima Prefecture, Ishikami Mura, a group of seven Sōka Gakkai men tore down a Kannon temple building and burned the image. Several men entered a Christian Church in Aomori Prefecture, and, when the minister would not convert, took his Bible and beat it on the floor. A man came home one day to his house on the island of Mukaishima to discover that his wife had thrown into the ocean a Buddhist altar which had been in his family for several generations. He left her immediately and instituted divorce proceedings. In November, 1964, three young men approached a housewife in her home when her husband was away on a business trip. The woman responded that she might perhaps be interested but that she wanted to talk it over with her husband. This encouraged the young men to press their advantage, and they made their way into the interior of the home, seized the Shintō and Buddhist worship objects which they found in the altar, and burned them. In Nemuro, Hokkaidō, on Christmas day, 1964, a man and his wife and two other adults, all members of Sōka Gakkai, called on a friend whose husband was in the hospital. According to the report the wife, after four hours of browbeating, finally signed her name to the roll. No sooner had she registered than the four callers began to rip out all the paraphernalia from the altar and god shelf, and burned it in the stove. The wife protested, saying that these things belonged to her mother, but her visitors insisted that the burning of the icons of false religions was her first act in her new faith.

Such is the fervor of Sōka Gakkai's iconoclasm. Recently, however, because of the constant recurrence of unreasonable acts of violence on the part of overly devout members and mounting public criticism, Sōka Gakkai has begun to modify the instruction regarding *hōbōbarai*. In the book published by the Tokyo University Sōka Gakkai group, already mentioned, the advice to members is in a much milder vein than that which appeared in Kodaira's earlier (1958) work, *Sōka Gakkai*. Moreover, in a book which came off the press in May, 1962, members were advised not to tear down god shelves or burn talismen and amulets before they had secured the consent of the other members of the family. Younger members, especially women, were advised that they might have to be content to let the god shelves remain in their homes if family members of higher status did not consent to their removal. Ancestral tablets, they are now told, do not have to be burned but must not be treated as objects of faith. And Shintō kami, in many cases the spirits of former rulers, great men, or pioneers who are enshrined throughout the country, can now receive respect but must not be worshiped.

The truth of the matter is that Sōka Gakkai leaders have never been happy about the public image that fanatical members —especially young members—have created, and they have consciously sought to change this image and gain as much respectability as possible for their organization. One way to achieve this, of course, is to persuade the press not to publish unfavorable reports, and it is understood that this has been done. The general director of a leading literary journal told this author in an interview that Sōka Gakkai was "quite noisy" about unsolicited news coverage in the secular press. It is easy to understand how a newspaper with a national circulation would be wary of offending a potential reading public of several million! Perhaps this may account for the "silent press . . . created during the last eight years," about which Kiyoaki Murata wrote in the *Japan Times* (June 11, 1964).

However, in spite of recent indications of a more conciliatory attitude, Sōka Gakkai continues to be intolerant of all other religions. On this point there is no evidence of any change of heart.

The *Shakubuku Kyōten* (Manual on Forced Conversions) is Sōka Gakkai's indispensable guide for conversion activity. In this one volume the member is given all that is considered necessary concerning the teachings of his own faith, as well as the essential characteristics of all other religions (in the area of interest of the Japanese). The points most vulnerable to attack in other religions are listed, and the faithful member has them all on the tip of his tongue. It is interesting for members of other faiths to talk to a number of members in entirely different situations and listen to them voicing the same criticisms. If the conversation advances one step beyond what they have been taught from the manual they are lost. It is a most sobering experience for a Christian missionary, such as the writer, to discover that apparently the sum total of all that these people know about Christianity is what is presented in their *Shakubuku Kyōten*. Probably the followers of other religious faiths feel the same way.

When the evil religions are destroyed by removing the source of disasters, and the True Religion is held by an entire nation, that nation and society will naturally become peaceful, secure, and rich.

(from *Risshō Ankokuron,* by Nichiren)

六章

RELIGION AND POLITICS

In order to learn directly from headquarters what the attitude of the leaders was toward one of their national political victories, I decided simply to write a letter asking for information. The response was instantaneous and totally unexpected, like the accidental detonation of a hidden land mine. Within the week a middle-aged, well-dressed gentleman appeared at my home and presented his card. He was head of the local district organization of Sōka Gakkai. It seems he had received a telephone call from headquarters in Tokyo, from no less a person than Mr. Shiraki, one of the councilors who had been successful in the election. The purpose of the visit to me, however, was not political but religious; and it was soon obvious that the caller was more interested in sealing a convert than in signing a supporter.

If the issues of politics and religion seem confused in this incident it is a confusion which emanates from the very heart of the matter; that is, in the guiding motivation of Sōka Gakkai itself. There is no contradiction to the believer; for the realms of politics and religion are not separate autonomous realms, but merely aspects of one unified reality.

Since its political debut in the local elections of 1955, followed by the placing of three candidates in the Upper House (House of Councilors) of the National Diet in 1956, Sōka Gakkai has advanced step by measured step into the arena of politics until it now has emerged as a full-blown political party. This progress has brought the Sōka Gakkai political arm (under the name of Kōmeitō, Clean Government Party), as a result of the Upper House election on July 7, 1968, to a strength of 24 (4 newly acquired) seats in the Upper House and 25 in the Lower House. The Kōmeitō is now acknowledged to be the third political power in the Japanese National Diet.

In preparation for the Upper House election in July, 1962, Sōka Gakkai politicians organized, in January, under the name "The League for Clean Politics" *(Kōmei Seiji Renmei)* with Diet member Kōji Harashima as chairman and eight other Diet and 310 local asemblymen members. The group, registered as the *Kōmeikai* (Clean Government Association), officially subscribed to a four-point platform: Opposition to nuclear weapons, protection of the "peace constitution," fair elections-clean politics, and establishment of the independence of the Upper House.[1] All nine Sōka Gakkai candidates ran on independent tickets since the group had not yet registered as a political party. A unanimous victory for Sōka Gakkai candidates resulted in the establishment of the group as a negotiation body within the National Diet. With six incumbents, Sōka Gakkai councilors reached a strength of fifteen, entitling them to enter as a recognized body into talks with counterparts on important parliamentary problems such as steering methods and the budget. On November 17, 1964, the Kōmeikai became Kōmeitō (Clean Government Party) signifying its establishment as a political party, and, in the Upper House election of 1965, Sōka Gakkai increased its strength to twenty to become the "Third Force" in the House of Councilors.

Though the Kōmeitō had never officially announced its intentions regarding the Lower House (House of Representatives) it was generally understood that Sōka Gakkai was content with representation in the Upper House alone. President Ikeda himself, in a press interview with the *Sandei Mainichi* (Sunday Mainichi), July 15, 1962, denied that Sōka Gakkai was eyeing Lower House seats. Consequently, the announcement on May 4, 1964, that Sōka Gakkai would run thirty candidates (names were listed) for the next Lower House election set off a tremor in the political world. Jōei Akiya, vice-chairman of the board of Sōka Gakkai, said the decision to run in the Lower House election was made because of strong demands from both "outside and within" Sōka Gakkai. Upon hearing this announcement the Liberal Democratic Party (majority party) claimed not to be affected in the least, but the Japan Socialist Party manifested some uneasiness and began to set up plans to counter the new Sōka Gakkai offensive. The concern of the Socialists no doubt stems from their recognition that

Sōka Gakkai's political candidates will steal their own fire in the campaigning since the platforms agree on such major points as (1) early recognition of Communist China, (2) recognition of Nationalist China, (3) early normalization of relations with the Republic of Korea (demanding the cutting of the Rhee Line), and (4) demands for the return of the Kurile Islands from the Soviet Union and Okinawa from the United States.

In politics which way does Sōka Gakkai lean—to the left or to the right?[2] In Japan this question usually means, "In matters of legislation, which party will the minority group of Sōka Gakkai councilors side with: the Liberal Democrats or the Socialists?" Sōka Gakkai president, Ikeda, has publicly denied that there is any fascist orientation to this organization, claiming that Sōka Gakkai is not prejudiced in favor of a People's Movement nor does it advocate a violent revolution. According to Ikeda, Sōka Gakkai calls for a "Peace Revolution" based on love (*jihi*), which is the spirit of the Buddhist Dharma.

1955 Local Elections

Sōka Gakkai in its first venture into politics in 1955 concentrated its efforts in Tokyo where Takashi Koizumi of the Board of Directors of this group was elected to the Tokyo Prefectural Assembly and thirty-three other Sōka Gakkai sponsored candidates were elected to ward assemblies. In city council elections six were successful in Kanawagawa Prefecture, five in Saitama, four in Miyagi, two in Chiba, and fifty-seven others throughout the country.

1956 House of Councilors Election

Sōka Gakkai nominated four candidates from the national constituency for the Upper House election of July 1, 1956— Takehisa Tsuji, head of the youth department; Shunpachi Hōjō, former member of the prewar House of Peers and adviser to the Sōka Gakkai culture department; Yoshihei Kodaira, head of the education department of Sōka Gakkai and former employee of the Labor ministry; and Kōji Harashima, the present chairman of the Board of Directors.

Successful were Tsuji, a native son of Hokkaidō who was

supported by a large anti-union bloc in the coal mining district of Yūbari and came in twenty-third with a total of 315,597 votes, and Hōjō, an older man (then 65 years old) who ranked forty-fourth of the total of 128 elected.

Two candidates ran in the local constituencies: Miss Yasu Kashiwabara who ended 37,000 votes short of the number needed for election in Tokyo, and Giichirō Shiraki, a former professional baseball player, who was sucessful in Ōsaka.

This election placed three Sōka Gakkai members in the House of Councilors of the National Diet.

1959 Local Elections

A total of 293 Sōka Gakkai candidates were elected to prefectural, city, and ward assemblies throughout the country. In the prefectural assembly elections they succeeded in placing only four.

1959 House of Councilors Election

The results of the 1959 Upper House election were sensational in that all six Sōka Gakkai candidates were elected, five from the national constituency and one from Tokyo. The Tokyo District election was bitterly contested, but Miss Kashiwabara, a primary school teacher and head of the Guidance Department of Sōka Gakkai (defeated in 1956), gained a spectacular victory with 471,472 votes—179,545 higher than the closest running candidate.

Tsugio Ishida, Tatsuyoshi Nakao, Yoshihei Kodaira, Kōji Harashima, and Hiroshi Ushida were elected from the national constituency. Ushida, chairman of the Youth Department of Sōka Gakkai, was the lowest ranking of the five candidates, but even he ran twenty-fourth of a total of fifty-two. This would seem to indicate that even more candidates could possibly have been successful.

Three of the successful candidates from the national constituency had run in previous elections and been defeated: Kodaira and Harashima in the 1956 Upper House election, and Nakao in the special election for an Ōsaka District councilor in 1957. Miss

Kashiwabara, running in the Tokyo District, had just missed election in 1956.

The success of Ishida (ranked fifth), who was hitherto unknown and only thirty-four years of age, was a clear testimony to the organizational power of Sōka Gakkai. He was at the time editor of the Sōka Gakkai newspaper, the *Seikyō Shinbun.*

1962 House of Councilors Election

Nine candidates running on independent tickets were backed by Sōka Gakkai in the July 1, 1962, Upper House election. There victory was assured, according to the *Sandei Mainichi* (Sunday Mainichi), July 15, by an unpaid constituency of 3,300,000 Sōka Gakkai followers, each responsible for two votes. It is not surprising that this victory of a religious group has elicited numerous comments, such as the following from the Japan Socialist Party: "It will not be an easy matter to thwart this Sōka Gakkai offensive, and it is a mistake to treat it lightly." Yoshiyuki Suzuki, vice-director of the Liberal Democrat election campaign, said, "There's nothing to fear from the Socialists, but lay down your arms [meaning "hats off"] to the new religions."

A comparison of the total number of votes gained in the 1962 election with the two previous Upper House elections is a good index to the increasing strength of Sōka Gakkai's political machine. From the national constituency it captured approximately 2,490,000 votes in 1959 compared to 990,000 votes in 1956. In the 1962 election, the seven national candidates received a total of 4,124,296 votes, or 11.5 percent of the votes cast. The Liberal Democratic Party captured 41.2 percent of the votes in 1959 and 46.4 percent in 1962, while the Socialist Party received 26.5 percent of the total in 1959. In 1962 the total Socialist vote was 29.5 percent of the total, but this was divided between the Socialist Party with 24.2 percent and the Social Democratic Party with 5.3 percent. The Ryokufūkai received 8.1 percent of the vote in 1959 but its replacement, the Dōshikai, dropped to 4.7 percent in 1962. The Communist Party rose from 1.9 percent in 1959 to 3.1 percent in 1962 while the independents declined from 19.8 to 15.5, with Sōka Gakkai alone accounting for 11.5 percent of this. It should also be noted that seven of the eight independents elected from the national constituency in 1962 were Sōka Gakkai candidates.

SŌKA GAKKAI CANDIDATES FROM THE NATIONAL CONSTITUENCY
July 1, 1962, House of Councilors Election

NAME	AGE	RANK	VOTES GARNERED
Tōru Asai	59	6	696,156
Shunpachi Hōjō	71	9	650,164
Kazuhiro Suzuki	37	10	629,363
Kunihiko Shibuya	38	13	603,093
Bunzō Ninomiya	42	14	595,724
Takehisa Tsuji	44	26	489,980
Katsutoshi Oniki	57	30	459,789

(Total number elected, 127)

The two candidates running in the local districts were equally successful. Satoru Izumi (age 51), a director of Sōka Gakkai and manager of the *Nihon Fujin Shinbun* (Japan Women's News), ran from the Tokyo District. In the wake of the 1959 record victory for the Tokyo District candidate, Miss Kashiwabara, his success was apparent from the beginning. He was especially strong in the outlying areas and slum districts of Tokyo.

Giichirō Shiraki, the professional baseball player who had been successful in the 1956 election, was re-elected in the Ōsaka District.

1963 Local Elections[3]

In the elections for prefectural assemblies and for ward, town, and village councils held respectively on April 17 and April 30, 1963, Sōka Gakkai succeeded in seating 971 of its 992 candidates, a record of 97.8 percent success. The main strength was shown in Tokyo where Sōka Gakkai took 17 of the 120 seats of the Tokyo Prefectural Assembly. Throughout the country, where Sōka Gakkai candidates ran for prefectural assemblies they usually placed first or second, with the exception of Ibaraki Prefecture in which the Sōka Gakkai candidate was defeated. In the city, town, and ward assemblies (not including here the Big Five: Tokyo, Yokohama, Nagoya, Kyoto, Ōsaka, Kōbe) 587 out of 604 Sōka Gakkai candidates were successful. As a result of these elections Sōka Gakkai increased in strength from a total of 293 in office in 1959 to 1,079, distributed as follows:

Prefectural Assemblies	56
City Councils	725
Ward Councils	137
Town and Village Councils	161
Total	1,079

1965 House of Councilors Election

Having been officially recognized as a political party, the Kōmeitō, backed by Sōka Gakkai, ran nine candidates from the national constituency and five from the prefectures, making a total of fourteen candidates. This was the first time Sōka Gakkai candidates had not run on independent tickets. A year prior to the election in July, 1965, fifteen candidates had been announced, but one of these (from the national constituency) died in the interval. All of the nine candidates from the national constituency were elected, but of the five prefectural candidates only the ones from Tokyo and Ōsaka were successful; candidates for Hyōgo, Fukuoka, and Aichi were defeated.

Though Sōka Gakkai captured a total of 5,090,000 votes and increased in strength from 13 (two of Sōka Gakkai's 15 councilors having died in office) to 20, still the Kōmeitō political machine showed signs of weakness in its first contest. For one thing, the spell of 100 percent success had been broken; for another, Sōka Gakkai's pivotal role in the Upper House had been relinquished to the potential accumulative one-third majority now residing in the combined strength of the Japan Socialist Party, the Japan Democratic Socialist Party, and the Communist Party.

A comparison of votes cast for Kōmeitō candidates with membership in Sōka Gakkai reveals a decreased ratio in vote-getting power of the organization. Taking the past four Upper House elections in which Sōka Gakkai has been involved, the results were as follows:

VOTE-GETTING POWER OF SŌKA GAKKAI

	MEMBERSHIP (by family units)	VOTES	RATIO
1956 Election	400,000	990,000	2.5 times
1959 Election	1,000,000	2,490,000	2.5 times
1962 Election	2,700,000	4,100,000	1.5 times
1965 Election	5,500,000	5,090,000	0.8 times

Of the total of 127 councilors elected, 71 were Liberal Democrats, 36 were Socialists, 11 were of the Kōmeitō, 3 were Communists, 3 Democratic Socialists, and 3 Independents.

1965 Tokyo Prefectural Assembly Election

The July 23, 1965, Tokyo Prefectural Assembly Election, following in the wake of the Upper House Election, constituted a resounding victory for the Socialists over the Liberal Democrats, and put Sōka Gakkai in a strategic position.

The results of the House of Councilors election a few days earlier clearly indicated the trend which the Tokyo election was to take. But it was the biggest upset in the history of the Liberal Democratic Party to have to relinquish the controlling majority in the 120-member legislative body of Japan's largest city (where one-tenth of the population lives) to the Socialists, and Sōka Gakkai played a leading role in unseating them. As a result of the election, the Liberal Democratic Party, which had formerly held 69 seats, now had 38, the Socialists had 45 seats, and the Kōmeitō had 23. Sōka Gakkai now has the decisive vote in the Tokyo Legislative Assembly.

The next step in strengthening its position in Tokyo politics would be a bid for the governor's spot. It was no surprise when this bid came, after the Lower House election in 1967, with the endorsement of Kenichi Abe by the Kōmeitō as a candidate to run in the April (1967) gubernatorial election in Tokyo. Mr. Abe is one of the directors of Sōka Gakkai.

1967 House of Representatives Election

"Black mist" (*kuroi kiri*) was ostensibly the issue of the House of Representatives election held on January 29, 1967. The non-Tory parties hoisted slogans: "Sweep out the black mist!" "Do away with rotten politics!" "Election purge!" The accusations were hurled at the Satō (Liberal Democrat) cabinet, and referred to public and private life scandals of certain cabinet members, graft in the Tokyo Assembly, a certain sugar industry scandal involving bribery, and other incidents. The success of the Kōmeitō in its first effort in the Lower House election may be attributed in large part to the effectiveness of the "black mist" campaign, though, surprisingly enough, the Liberal Democrats who controlled with 278 seats before came out with a total of 277 in the new Diet.

With 486 seats in the Lower House at stake, the final election results appeared on January 31 as follows:

HOUSE OF REPRESENTATIVES ELECTION
January 29, 1967

	Seats Secured	Candidates	Predissolution Strength
Liberal Democrats	277	342	278
Socialists	140	209	141
Democratic Socialists	30	60	23
Kōmeitō	25	32	0
Communists	5	123	4
Minor Parties	0	16	1
Independents	9	135	1
Total . . .	486	917	448 (38 seats vacant)

Following the election the Kōmeitō called a convention for February 13 and replaced the chairman and secretary general with newly elected representatives. Yoshikatsu Takeiri replaced Takahisa Tsuji as chairman, and Junya Yano replaced Hiroshi Hōjō as secretary general. The former, Mr. Takeiri, had been elected from the tenth district of Tokyo, and Mr. Yano had been elected from the fourth district of Ōsaka.

Let us turn our attention now to a consideration of some of the factors contributing to the success of Sōka Gakkai's political venture.

The Popular Vote

Commenting on the victory of Sōka Gakkai in the 1962 election Masamichi Inoki, professor of law at Kyōto University, said this result was more of a protest against the antiquated established parties than anything else. In a reporters' round table review of the election, one reporter for the newspaper *Asahi* remarked that since the largest voting bloc for Sōka Gakkai was from among the lower-middle industrial class to which the rescuing hand of the reform groups had not yet reached, the victory was to be attributed to the neglect of the reform camps.

Others have attributed Sōka Gakkai's phenomenal show of political strength to its success in catching votes falling in between the Liberal Democrats and the Socialists. The strongest voting for Sōka Gakkai clearly comes from the "floating vote" of the large cities. While the capitalists expect something from the Liberal Democrats, and big labor interests centering in Sōhyō look to the Socialists, it is Sōka Gakkai which has appealed to the little man lost in the gap between these two big interests.

The Machine

It is no doubt the tight, efficient organization of Sōka Gakkai itself, however, that has brought about the amazing success of the Kōmeitō. The intimate relationship between the backing religious organization and the political party is no secret to anyone. Though the Kōmeitō now claims 100,000 party members and approximately 2,000 ranking legislators, the real power is in its backer, Sōka Gakkai. One has only to look at the directors list for each organization in Sōka Gakkai and compare the names with Kōmeitō leaders to see that central figures play dual roles. Tsuji, who was committee chairman of Kōmeitō, is also Vice-Chairman of the Board of Sōka Gakkai. Hōjō was both General Secretary of the Kōmeitō and Chairman of the Board for Sōka Gakkai. Though Ikeda does not appear on the Kōmeitō roster of directors he can make such remarks as: "If ever there develops a faction within the party we will have it dissolved."

From the beginning Sōka Gakkai has meant *organization*. Some have referred to it as "militaristic," because of the use of such terms as "squad" and "troop," and because of militaristic reviews, and so forth, or as "communistic," because of the numerous cell units.

A few years ago the organizational structure was modified to include a horizontal relationship, called "blocks" (transliteration of the English word "block"), which in fact has a stronger influence on the individual member than the vertical relationship to group, squad, district, area, and so forth. The "block" is a geographic unit. The smallest block is made up of some twenty to thirty households in a given area. It may be that the members are also members of some other group or squad in another area, but this does not matter. Under the new organization they have a dual affiliation. This has been called the "railroad track" organization, because the two affiliations run parallel. "Minor blocks" are incorporated into what is called simply "block"; then these are incorporated into a "major block," a "general block," and finally, the "unified general block."

The significance of this organizational method in politics began to come to light in the 1959 election. The national headquarters of Sōka Gakkai divided the national constituency into five geographical blocs, assigning each a candidate. An analysis of the vote shows that this strategy was carefully followed, for in most prefectures from ninety to ninety-five percent of the Sōka Gakkai vote was concentrated on a single candidate.

In the 1962 election this pattern was also observed. Tsuji, for example, had almost imperceptible support outside of Hokkaidō and northern Honshū. Asai hardly averaged a thousand votes each in districts outside of the Ōsaka area. Oniki, for example, did not receive even a hundred votes each in fifteen districts, but of the 127 elected councilors he was the only candidate in six figures in Fukuoka. Thus, it appears, each of the seven national candidates was assigned to one of the seven strategic geographical districts: Hokkaidō-Tōhoku, Kanagawa-Gunma, Tokyo, Shizuoka-Aichi, Ōsaka-Hyōgo, Hiroshima, and Fukuoka. This same strategy was followed in the 1965 election when Kōmeitō assigned nine candidates to nine different districts.

Moreover, the *Seikyō Shinbun* (propaganda organ for Sōka Gakkai) was clearly utilized as a means to disseminate political propaganda. Candidates were introduced and their platforms outlined in this newspaper. Public rallies, ostensibly religious meetings, were quite obviously used by candidates for their political campaigning. The *Shūkan Asahi* (Weekly Asahi), June 6, 1959, pointed out the strategy of Sōka Gakkai in calling one of these "religious" rallies before the official opening of the campaign period. In a mass meeting in Ōsaka which 100,000 Sōka Gakkai members attended, the candidate for election, Nakao, was introduced as the principal "lecturer." He didn't speak about the election, but from the ovation given him by the crowd it was clear that he had made his point and his bid for their votes. Sōka Gakkai candidates had the backing of every member of the society. Numerous incidents of the somewhat amusing antics of overly devout supporters were reported in the 1962 election. Some believers, considering it sacrilegious that a Sōka Gakkai candidate's placard should get wet in the rain, scouted through the town covering them all with plastic. Ōsaka taxicab drivers considered each fare an opportunity to push a candidate. One reporter, covering a story on Sōka Gakkai, himself underwent the experience of being harangued by an Ōsaka cab driver who parroted the society's propaganda slogan: "Liberal Democrats mean inflationary prices; Democratic Socialists are opportunists; and Communists are Russia's flunkies." When the reporter paid his fare he was given a copy of the *Seikyō Shinbun*. In a public lecture meeting at the Tokyo Shinjuku Hall where candidates of all parties appeared, Sōka Gakkai members appeared en masse to drown out with noise any candidate not supported by their own group. An estimated 5.5 million members (or households) are organized into a forceful propaganda machine, which, according to President Ikeda, do not receive one yen from the organization for their services. In election time, Sōka Gakkai candidates made the rounds in Japanese-made three-wheelers while their opponents rode in comfortable limousines, a technique more related to vote gathering, no doubt, than to lack of campaign funds.

Election Law Violations

With all this political fervor it was inevitable that some supporters would overstep the boundaries of legal campaigning. Serious offenses were committed in 1956, prompting the police to raid the local headquarters looking for incriminating evidence. According to the newspaper *Asahi,* June 25, 1956, twenty leaders were taken to police headquarters and questioned on suspicion of having broken the election law against house-to-house canvassing. In Kanagawa alone the police reported 230 suspects. Violations were especially great among Sōka Gakkai supporters, who according to the police report of a national survey, accounted for eighty percent of the violations of this law. Offenders were apprehended in Kyōto, Ōsaka, Hachiōji, Miyagi, Aomori, Tochigi, Saitama, Tokyo, and many other places. In Ōsaka alone 110 Sōka Gakkai members, including leaders, were indicted.

Election law violations were even greater in the 1957 special election for a councilor from the Ōsaka District. Over ninety percent of those arrested for violations in this election were members of Sōka Gakkai. Takashi Koizumi, assemblyman from Tokyo, was arrested for distributing cigarettes, hundred yen bills, and boxes of caramels with the candidate Nakao's name printed on them. These were given to unemployed persons standing before the employment office the day before the election. The present president of Sōka Gakkai, Ikeda, was arrested in this election but was soon released without charge.

In the 1959 election Sōka Gakkai leaders had evidently taken some pains to indoctrinate overzealous supporters, for the number of violations among members of the society was negligible. The *Shūkan Asahi* (Weekly Asahi), June 6, 1959, reported eleven cases, mostly violations of the law prohibiting talking to people outside the polls.

A few election law violations came to light after the 1962 election. Mrs. Ninomiya, wife of a successful candidate, was questioned for election law violation but charges were soon dropped. In Kōchi Prefecture, of six apprehended on charges of violation of the election law four were Sōka Gakkai members campaigning for Ninomiya. One case each of offending Sōka Gakkai members was reported in Kyōto and in Shiga Prefecture. In an article reporting on the total of 342 violations following this election (*Asahi,* July 4, 1962) the reporter voiced a suspicion which has been generally current concerning the 1962 House of Councilors election, to the effect that some Sōka Gakkai members illegally registered in order to strengthen the vote in specified districts. According to this report Sōka Gakkai men were held on suspicion of having voted up to three times. At that time the current opinion was that Sōka Gakkai members had been encouraged to move their voting registration to a new district well in advance of the three-month limit, so that the vote distribution would be in favor of their own candidate.

An illustration of violent action connected with elections is to be noted in the following article printed in the *Asahi*, June 17, 1962:

> Two officers of the Youth Department of Sōka Gakkai headquarters in Tokyo were arrested by the Yotsuya police on the charge of violation of the Election Law (Article 225) in the House of Councilors Election (July, 1962). Supporters of a candidate were broadcasting criticism of Sōka Gakkai from a campaign car when thirty members of the Youth Department came out of the Shinanomachi national headquarters of Sōka Gakkai and set up a chant to obstruct the campaign speeches. The campaigners were manhandled and the microphone was put out of commission. Two representatives, Ogawa and Fujiwara, of the fifty-eight apprehended were detained for questioning on the charge of obstructing legal political campaigning.

Some members complain that they have been unduly singled out for investigation in connection with election law violations, and not without some justification. As the election law stands, there are a number of fine points on which a person could be accused of violation but which are commonly ignored, such as making lunches for campaigners. Sōka Gakkai members say that they have been watched intently while other groups have been allowed to operate freely. On July 17, 1962, three young men stormed a police station in Kyōto and attacked and injured four policemen in protest of unfair treatment regarding election law violations.

Political Motive

What is behind all this political frenzy? While election campaigning is no doubt a ready escape valve for the unspent energy of Japan's restive youth, and there is enormous potential in Sōka Gakkai's membership of 900,000 in the Youth Department and 750,000 in the Young Women's Department, still there is more to this political activity than emotional release. Sōka Gakkai's involvement in politics has its roots in the basic teachings of the organization, and in the teachings of Nichiren himself.

Nichiren was directly involved in the politics of his day. Openly defying the Hōjō regents in the Kamakura capital, Nichiren warned that unless false religions were suppressed and the True Dharma espoused, the nation itself would be destroyed. In the *Risshō Ankokuron* he wrote that the ruler was giving misguided government and that for this reason the good kami had left Japan. He called upon the emperor and rulers of the land to adopt the True Buddhist Doctrine in order to avoid natural calamities and a foreign invasion.

Toda, in his commentary on this writing of Nichiren, drew parallels between the religious, social, and political condition of Japan in the Kamakura period and today. Evidence that the good kami have left and the evil demons have invaded Japan today are to be found, for example, in the high price of grain (rice is 1,000 times the prewar price); foreign invasion is only too obvious with the loss of World War II and the present dependence upon resident foreign troops (the time of Toda's writing was 1952); pestilence is manifest everywhere, not only in physical but also in spiritual sickness, for delinquency and schizophrenia are also a type of pestilence. Thus Toda interpreted Nichiren's prophecies in terms of the conditions of Japan in his day. According to him these conditions correspond to the three evils of the *Mahā-sannipata Sūtra*.

Other similarities to the calamities mentioned in this *sūtra* are listed by Toda as follows: (1) The good kami have left Japan. ("During the last war we worshiped Amaterasu, but to no avail.") (2) The King gives orders but the people do not obey. ("Look at our Emperor! He is a king with no power. But the basis for his loss of power was not, as some suppose, defeat in the war. It was because the Buddhist Dharma had been abandoned.") (3) The country will be invaded by foreign armies. ("It is not necessary to comment on this!") (4) The occurrence of great fires. ("Consider the fires of the last war. Even now in days of peace there are an exceptional number of destructive fires.") (5) Evil winds and great waters. ("Think of the disastrous typhoons!") (6) Internecine strife. ("Consider the Korean War, the Taiwan problem, the struggle over Okinawa, Sakhalin, and the Kuriles.") (7) The King becomes ill, dies, and falls into the Great Hades. ("The fact that the ruler has no power is his Great Illness. Let us pray for his healing. To this end we have prepared the special Worship Object which is to be given to the Emperor when he shall have been won to the true faith.") (8) The King's family, his retainers, the leaders of the government, all will fall sick, die, and enter into the Great Hades. ("Tōjō, the great leader during the last war, was imprisoned and put to death. When one considers the leaders of our land today, the members of the cabinet, city mayors, and so forth, they do not compare with the leaders of the Meiji period. They are weak. They have fallen ill. This is because they do not keep the Buddhist Dharma.")

Unity of Religion and State

Nichiren taught that the time would come when the law of the king and the Buddhist Dharma (or "law of Buddha") would become one. When this time comes the altar will be established at the Vulture Peak (identified as the temple Taisekiji at the foot of Mt. Fuji) and the true doctrine will be propagated throughout the earth. This teaching of the unity of religion and government expounded by Toda in the *Ōbutsu Myōgōron* (Theory of the Unity of Government and Religion) has been made one of the central teachings of Sōka Gakkai. Members believe that the time has now come for the establishment of the National Altar and for the unity of religion (the Nichiren Shō faith) and government.

According to the *Ōbutsu Myōgōron,* as long as there is confusion in the religion of a country there will be confusion in the government. Government is a technique. The function of government is to achieve a condition which fosters happiness for the citizen. The means by which government achieves this is through order and regulations. Religion, on the other hand, if it is true religion, removes the barriers to happiness. The *true religion,* as taught by or discovered by Nichiren, removes unhappiness and achieves a union of government and religion, both working toward the complete happiness (or fortune) of the individual.

The motive behind Sōka Gakkai involvement in politics, then, can be expressed in this word *ōbutsu myōgō* (literally "king-buddha unified," or "unity of the law of the king and the Buddhist Dharma") which the leaders define as "the establishment of the highest cultural state which actualizes this ancient government ideal"; namely, the achievement of happiness for the individual. At this point the Japan Socialist Party is attacked, for they say that even if this party were to carry through its promise of yen 6,000 for the aged, or the abolishment of nuclear tests, these are all aimed at some vague "social" improvement and will not affect the happiness of the individual. Unity of religion and government, according to Sōka Gakkai theory, will be a-political; i.e., no particular party such as the Socialist, the Democratic, or People's parties, will be necessary. It is not a religious party which these members are seeking to establish, but a religious nation. (Note the name, Kōmeitō, "Clean Government Party.") It is little wonder, then, that Toshiyoshi Miyazawa, professor of law at Rikkyō University, expressed the fear that with such an uncompromising attitude on the part of Sōka Gakkai, if it were to gain power in the government the entire democratic foundation of the nation would be shaken.

Koizumi, Sōka Gakkai director, has made the political motive of this organization clear: "Our purpose is to purify the world through the propagation of the teaching of the Nichiren Shō Denomination. Twenty years from now we will occupy the majority of seats in the National Diet and establish the Nichiren Shō Denomination as the national religion of Japan and construct a national altar at Mt. Fuji. This is the sole and ultimate purpose of our association." The year 1979 is prophesied to be the year in which this purpose will be consummated.

Election Pledges

The Kōmeikai presented a four-plank platform in the 1962 House of Councilors Election: (1) Opposition to nuclear weapons, (2) opposition to the amendment of the Peace Constitution, (3) purification of the political world, and (4) establishment of a more independent Upper House.

Candidates in general carried the party line, adding here and there innocuous pledges which seem to have been designed to capture votes from the Democratic Socialists: promotion of Japan-China trade; return of Okinawa from the United States and Sakhalin and the Kuriles from Soviet Russia; increased emigration. Other items appealed no doubt to the average Sōka Gakkai vote: simplification of the taxation system; abolition of workers' income tax; tax cut for medium and small scale industries, farmers, and fishermen; modernization of medium and small enterprises; development of forestry and fishery industries; renovation of the educational structure; promotion of a social security system; solution of the housing problem; revamping of the anti-disaster system; solution of the traffic problem; solution of the labor problems.

Significantly the Sōka Gakkai candidates advocated the establishment of a Culture Ministry in the government. It remains to be seen whether this has relation to their plans to gain control of religious activities through this agency in a manner similar to the control exerted by the Ministry of Education during World War II. It is also interesting to note that the call for a Culture Ministry did not appear in the platforms of other candidates besides Sōka Gakkai.

The Kōmeitō's Role in National Politics

Up till now Sōka Gakkai councilors (in the Upper House) have made no distinctive contribution to any particular piece of legislation, but have followed, in general, the policies of the conservatives (that is, Liberal Democrats). For example, in the pamphlet called "Sōka Gakkai" put out by the Japan Socialist Party, Sōka Gakkai voting behavior on important bills was revealed. In the thirty-eighth and thirty-ninth sessions of the Diet the Japan Socialist Party voted against fifty-six of the 238 laws passed, while the Social Democrats voted against thirty-four. Sōka Gakkai, however, voted against only five, and these were bills relating to defense and increased prices. In the fortieth Diet session (December, 1961 to May, 1962) Sōka Gakkai voted against eleven of the 166 cabinet proposals. In addition it should be noted that its councilors voted against three budget proposals which are directly connected with tax levies on private individuals.

Kōmeitō's new chairman, Takeiri, sees his party as the only true "middle-of-the-road" party in Japan today—the only "People's Party." He reiterates the Kōmeitō's four basic principles: (1) Absolute pacificism, (2) Opposition to revision of the Constitution, (3) Abandonment of nuclear warfare, and (4) Realization of a social welfare state based upon a middle-of-the-road political policy. Kōmeitō candidates have promised that, if elected, they would infuse a new atmosphere into the Diet. This is the origin of the name, Kōmeitō (literally, "a party for fair and clean politics"). Already Kōmeitō councilors have taken a stand opposing the Liberal-Democratic stand on a very important issue; i.e., revision of the Peace Constitution. (Japan's Constitution is referred to, in Japan, as the "Peace Constitution" because of the provision in Chapter II, Article 9, which reads in part, ". . . the Japanese people forever renounce war as a sovereign right of the nation. . . ."). On this issue the Kōmeitō councilors have stood with Socialists and Communists. But on another crucial issue, the United States-Japan Mutual Security Treaty, according to a leading religious critic, Akio Sagi, the Kōmeitō talks double-talk; namely, the Kōmeitō opposes the revision of Article 9 of the Constitution which renounces Japan's right to arm herself for war while at the same time sponsoring the treaty on mutual security between Japan and the United States, which stipulates that Japan will go to war if the United States is attacked and vice versa.

The secular orientation of the state in Japan is underlined by Article 20 of the Constitution as follows: "No religious organization shall receive any privileges from the state, nor exercise any political authority." In view of the continued penetration of the government by a religious party, the Kōmeitō, the public has justifiable cause for alarm. As if to assuage this growing feeling of concern on the part of the general public, Chairman Takeiri made a statement to the press (*Shūkan Yomiuri,* February 17, 1967) as follows:

We are the very group most desirous of religious freedom! Before the war the Nichiren Shō Denomination was absolutely suppressed. We would never think of persecuting other religious faiths.

After the success of the January 29, 1967, House of Representatives election, a new chairman for the Kōmeitō was selected. He is Yoshikatsu Takeiri, councilor elected to the Lower House (age 42). The Secretary General for Kōmeitō is Jun'ya Yano. Ken'ichi Abe (Kōmeitō) lost his bid for governor of Tokyo in 1967, and political strength of Kōmeitō at the end of 1967 looked something like this:

Lower House 25
Upper House 20
Prefectural Assemblies
(including Tokyo, Ōsaka, Kyoto, Hokkaidō) 107
Ward and City Councils 1,317
Town and Village Councils ....about 2,000

President Ikeda (Sōka Gakkai) has outlined the policy of the Kōmeitō under the following headings:

1. Humane Middle-of-the-Road Policy
        —respect for the dignity of every individual.
        —middle-of-the-road between communism and a free competitive system; Ikeda calls it a "quasi-socialistic economic system."
2. A System of Welfare Economy
3. Social Security for the Majority
4. Opposition to Nuclear Weapons
        —ban production of nuclear weapons.
        —support and strengthen the security functions of the U.N.
        —dissolve the Japan-U.S. Mutual Security Treaty in the next ten to twenty years.
5. Ideal Party Politics
6. Guarantee of "Freedom of Religion"

On the occasion of the Sasebo incident over the *Enterprise,* the chairman of the Kōmeitō, Takeiri, announced that Kōmeitō had taken a new turn—from theory to action. Kōmeitō (and Sōka Gakkai) actively demonstrated in protest against the docking of the nuclear-powered aircraft carrier from the United States.

It may be that the Kōmeitō will eventually emerge as the chief opponent of the Liberal Democrat Party. It seems likely that this religious party will supplant the Japan Socialist Party in the public eye, for the latter has obviously injured its reputation by giving way to manifestations of leftist extremism of a sort palpably detrimental to Japan's best interests.

But the attentive observer of motives and trends within both the religious and the political organizations of Sōka Gakkai, which are specifically directed to the goal of establishment of Nichiren Shō Buddhism as "The National Cult of Japan," will not be immediately convinced by the campaign promise of the new political boss, Takeiri: "We would never think of persecuting other religious faiths."

Yoku mireba
nazuna hana saku
kakine kana

If one looks closely
a *nazuna* bud is opening
under the hedge

(A haiku poem by Bashō)

七章 THEORY, DOCTRINE, AND FAITH

That Sōka Gakkai was inspired by a schoolteacher who was also a student of the *Lotus Sūtra* is a fact of history which one is tempted to describe as a portentous coincidence. "Correct" teaching, handed down from above in the traditional oriental manner from *Sensei* to disciple—authoritative pronouncement and regimented obeisance—is a supporting pillar of the Japanese society. In Sōka Gakkai, though emphasis is placed heavily on deference to the teaching authority (*Sensei,* teacher) and invincible trust in the ultimacy of the Faith Object, nevertheless there is a theoretical rationale underlying the basic thought structure of the society. In Sōka Gakkai a strange wedding has taken place—a fusion of occidental utilitarianism and oriental mysticism. But no other development in postwar Japanese thought so dramatically portrays the inevitable meeting of East and West as does the movement of Sōka Gakkai. Strange inconsistencies, irreconcilable contradictions—perhaps these are the antecedents to Sōka Gakkai's development of the secularization of the Dharma. But to the Sōka Gakkai follower, at least, his Western philosophical theories and his oriental religious doctrines have become fused in the mystery of the incantation of the magic prayer, *Namu Myōhō-rengekyō.*

The Theory of Value[1]

Makiguchi's theory of value (developed in his posthumous book, *Kachiron*) claims to be a correction of the alleged aberrations of the traditional platonic values—truth, goodness, and beauty—by the substitution of the concept of "benefit" for that of "truth." The reason for this is said to be that truth and value are entirely different concepts. Truth reveals that which is; value connotes a subject-object relationship. Truth makes epistemological statements about an object. Value relates the object to man. Truth says, "Here is a horse"; value says, "The horse is beautiful." Truth remains truth regardless of any human relationship. Truth is unchanging. Value, on the other hand, is altered by time and space.

Truth is not a creation but a postulate, remaining always as that which is, that which is discovered. Value, on the other hand, is created. There remain, in fact, innumerable values which may still be created. All the materials man uses in his daily life are the products of nature; they are postulated in nature. Through the centuries, by man's own effort and for his own benefit, these have been improved and transformed into the forms and shapes in which we know them to exist today. This is what is meant, in Sōka Gakkai, by the term *"sōka"* (value creation).

"Creation" involves the discovery of a relationship between nature and man, evaluating it, and by human effort making that relationship relevant. Man alters nature to make it beneficial to him. By this definition "creation" is a term applicable only to value; it is not relevant to "truth."

Thus man creates values, and in this lies man's greatness. Man finds happiness—the goal of human life—in the pursuit of value. Happiness is the ideal state which is realized by means of the possession of values. Scientific history is the record of value creation and the relationship of these values to man's culture.

Truth and value are concepts of different realms. The truth or falsehood of a thing or an occurrence cannot be decided upon the basis of human emotion or sentiment. At times human emotion will reject the true and believe the false. Similarly, the true-false realm does not coincide with the good-evil realm. Because a thing is true does not make it good, nor is the false to be equated with evil. Sometimes the true is evil to man; sometimes the false is good. For example, a man hears the rumor of an earthquake and fire. If the rumor is substantiated it is not good to him, but evil. If the rumor is proven to be false, it is good.

In like manner it can be proven that the true-false realm is distinct from the two other values, beauty and benefit. Truth and falsehood have their independent existence apart from their effect upon man, but the values beauty-ugliness, good-evil, benefit-harm, are determined in the context of their relation to the evaluating subject.

The two separate realms of truth and value may be charted as follows:

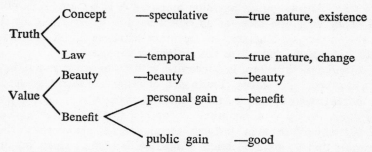

Truth	Concept	—speculative	—true nature, existence
	Law	—temporal	—true nature, change
Value	Beauty	—beauty	—beauty
	Benefit	personal gain	—benefit
		public gain	—good

Pragmatism is a mistaken philosophy because it confuses truth and value. To say "true value" is to imply that the opposite —that is, "false value" or "mistaken value"—also exists. Actually, truth neither manifests nor contains value. Pragmatism, however, claims that truth and value are alike and equal. Pragmatism is based on the false premise that if a thing is true it is beneficial to man. This premise is not borne out in experience. In fact, some things are true which are of no benefit to man at all. Ultimately the investigation of truth must be made irrespective of its usefulness to man.

Truth is unchanging. Though the Copernican theory seemed to upset the truth, actually it only upset false theories concerning the truth. Truth and the common law which controls the universe are essentially one and the same thing. The Copernican theory itself is not the truth but only the explanation of that common law which is fixed and unchanging.

But values change. Since values are the product of the relation between an object and a subject, if either of these factors changes then the value itself changes. The eternal argument started between Socrates and the Sophists has echoed until this very day. Socrates held that truth is unchanging; the Sophists held that man is the measure of all things. This conflict can be resolved only when we realize that the realm of truth and the realm of value are separate.

Evaluation is consciousness of the influence which an object has upon the subject. Cognition is the grasping of the meaning of an impression. Evaluation, therefore, is subjective; cognition is objective. For example, cognition asserts, "A is B," or "A is not C." Thus cognition receives an object as it is without relating it to the subject. Evaluation, on the other hand, says, "A is beautiful," etc., and relates it to the evaluating subject.

Cognition, therefore, is concerned with truth while evaluation is concerned with values. Truth is a qualitative concept grasped by intellectual response to the stimuli of phenomena; that is, by cognition. Value is a quantitative concept relating the influence of phenomena to man through emotional and intellectual responses; that is, by evaluation. Cognition is mental reception or intellectual activity; evaluation is sense perception or feeling response.

Cognition comes by the relation of a new perception to a past experience. Kant says that man perceives by *a priori* standards; but the truth is that man first decides whether something is the "same or different" on the basis of his experience. It isn't necessary to adopt the method of some philosopher (such as Kant) when we have the time-tested method of "same or different."

The relation of cognition to external phenomena we call "experience." This term "experience" is defined to mean the sensual, intellectual connection of subject and object. The relation of evaluation to external phenomena we call "intercourse." Intercourse is defined as the emotional, sentimental connection of subject and object. In the case of the former the external world has its independent existence and is not directly connected with our personal world. In the case of the latter the external world has a vital, intimate connection with our world. The latter is like the meeting of lovers:

> My love,
> though I try to hide it,
> shows in my face, until
> people begin
> to question.[2]

No matter how they may try to suppress their feelings for one another, lovers cannot deny or escape the influence of each other.

In order to know the external world it is necessary to employ both cognition and evaluation. If either is neglected one's understanding is incomplete. But science has pursued the objective method of cognition, and has analyzed and classified phenomena until we are left with only the pieces. This is why Bergson contends that science cannot get beyond the outer wall.

The truth is that cognition and evaluation do not need to be in conflict. When they appear to conflict in describing phenomena, it is essentially only a conflict arising out of the opposition of the whole to the parts, and not a basic conflict at all.

The ability to determine values is a human attribute. An object touches us; we react. This is a value judgment. There are thus three relationships between object and subject: non-value, when an object has no value to anyone; value, when an object has value to someone; and non-value, when value is ascribed to something that has no intrinsic value.

There are three values: beauty, benefit, and goodness. The value "beauty" is an emotional value relative only to a part of man's life. It is a temporary value appropriated through one or more of the five sense organs. The value "benefit" is an individual, personal value relative to the whole of man's life. It describes the relationship which the individual has with an object that contributes to maintaining and advancing human life. The value "goodness" is a social value relative to the life of the group. It describes the meaningful acts which man performs that contribute to the formation and development of a unified society; that is, goodness is equivalent to the public benefit.

Marx and other economists have said: "All which has utility is wealth." But Marx confuses value and wealth. Others have confused property and wealth. Property is anything of utility which man possesses. Wealth is the accumulation of property for the satisfaction of human desires. *Benefit* concerns the extent to which property has importance to man. Man can create benefit by arranging all factors so that they will contribute to his well-being.

Goodness, the good-evil concept, is a concept which belongs exclusively to the social group; it is not a personal value. The term "good" is equivalent to the term "group benefit." Instinct, man's common life-drive, is the absolute standard for judging all values. However, man possesses not only individual instinct but also the herd instinct. Therefore, social evaluation is necessary; but the common benefit of the mass cannot be the maximum benefit, it must be the lowest common denominator. The common benefit of the mass is only objective and negative. Thus moral value (good-evil) is fixed by the negative criterion: not desirable for the masses.

In contrast to this, however, is the Western adage, "Do unto others as you would have them do unto you." This is not based on the lowest common denominator and, thus, does not have universal validity or appropriateness. The personal standard of what is good for one cannot be forced onto another. This is certainly not a scientific standard for morality. On the other hand, the Eastern adage, "Do not do to others what you do not want them to do to you," is a truth which science can accept, since it is based on the lowest common denominator. It is possible to set a line below which all men can say, "This is undesirable." Hence, the Eastern adage has universal validity, and, as such, is scientific.

Socrates says that the purpose of action is not to achieve pleasure but to attain good. How does he measure good and evil? The answer is, when a thought is right it is good; when it is not right it is evil. The Socrates-Plato idea is: pleasure and good are not to be equated. Pleasure is pursued for the sake of good. If we, or things, are good this is only because we, or things, possess some virtue. But we cannot agree with this idea. If the sense of right judges the good, and if all things possess this sense, then we are left with the question: what is right? That by which we judge right and wrong is not truth but the general benefit (as opposed to individual benefit).

As for good, the individualist defines this as love of others. The ancient Greek said good equals might. Thus we see that the concept of good has changed with social history. The one fact which does not change is that good has its background in society. Good is therefore a social value.

That which reaches us through an object of the senses belongs to the value *beauty,* which is a temporary, sensory value. But the aesthetic object is not limited to physical phenomena. Experience tells us that beauty can be found elsewhere, as, for example, in human behavior. However, beautiful behavior is not equivalent to good behavior, nor is ugly behavior to be equated with bad. The fact that a thing is ugly or morally bad does not prevent it from having an aesthetic value. The standard, then, even for aesthetic value, is the judgment of whether or not a thing is beneficial to man.

* * *

The above is a summary of the argument of Makiguchi's *Kachiron,* or Theory of Value. As the founding principle of Sōka Gakkai the importance of this theory cannot be overestimated. It has been made the authoritative statement for the Sōka Gakkai interpretation of the meaning of human life and a standard against which to judge the validity of all religious faiths. It is used by the members as proof of the scientific validity of their own faith. For the scholarly, Makiguchi's book is an intellectual challenge. Non-intellectuals are satisfied to be conversant with a paraphrase of these ideas which appears as chapter 4, "Happiness and Life's Objective," in the *Shakubuku Kyōten.*

Though the *Kachiron* as it stands is ascribed to Makiguchi, it was compiled after his death by his successor, Toda, from a series of articles titled *"Sōka Kyōikugaku Taikei."* However, there are a number of inconsistencies in its argument which lead to the inescapable conclusion that the editor took great liberties in bringing what may have been originally a purely utilitarian philosophical treatise into conformity with the teachings of the Nichiren Shō faith.

Such inconsistencies had already occurred to me before I discovered a book called *Sōka Gakkai Hihan* (Criticism of Sōka Gakkai), which was published in 1955 by the rival Nichiren Denomination. The gist of this criticism is that the argument in *Kachiron* follows logical lines to the end of the chapter entitled

"What is Religious Value?" but then the reader turns the page to find that the author "haughtily defies" the reader and brings a complete stop to the process of reason.

Wholly extraneous material seems to have been forcibly wedged into an otherwise coherent argument. The section called "Standards of Religious Value" is a case in point. It begins:

> Why, at this point, is it necessary to discuss religion? It is because value and happiness, the object of this treatise, absolutely cannot be considered apart from religion. Furthermore, scholars up to now, as well as the ordinary people, have not known how to judge religion in the light of the evaluation standard of beauty-ugliness, benefit-harm, good-evil, and so have all been led astray by religion and fallen into suffering and despair, failing to grasp the happiness which they sought. One has no right to talk about happiness if he is ignorant of religion, or, seeing it only partially, is under the illusion that he has grasped the whole.
>
> Religion is believing (and acting on this belief) that the object of faith has the values beauty, benefit, and goodness, even though the individual himself cannot judge through his own intelligence.[3]

This last sentence (in the translation) is a direct refutation of the entire preceding section, "The Creation of Personal Value," in which no mention is made of "belief" but value creation seems to be entirely in man's power to control. Contrast, also, the following two quotations:

> Venderband, in addition to truth, goodness, and beauty, distinguished a value called holiness, and set it up as a religious value. Many philosophers who follow this stream of thought think it impossible to establish a system of value without this classification. But where is there any grounds for establishing a religious value?
>
> Does not this condition of calm resignation which man reaches when he has been saved from the burden of life's extremity correspond to the social value of morality which we have postulated? Or, if it is viewed from the personal standpoint, is this not the same as the value of benefit? There is no social meaning to religion outside its reference to the salvation of man or the salvation of the world. The salvation of man is benefit value, and the salvation of the world is the value

goodness. Whether we call it reward (*kudoku*) or merit (*gori-yaku*), we may use an elegant word but the content of these words is the same. . . . I repeat, after all we cannot distinguish any other values than the values benefit, goodness, and beauty.[4]

The following quotation is a direct refutation of the above:

> There are some who deny the kami and buddhas and say they can live by their own conscience and faith. Or, they say, since they cannot have faith in anything save themselves, it is enough to live believing in self. . . . But nothing is as undependable as a man's conscience, especially in Japan. . . . The answer is in Buddhism's doctrine of ultimate reason, "the three thousand worlds exist in one intent thought of the mind" (*ichinensanzen*). . . . Man has in himself the basis for existing in all the three thousand worlds; man can realize the budda-world in this human world. . . . Man cannot "know thyself" unless he faces the Worship Object of Nichiren.[5]

Whatever may have been the original argument of the *Kachiron,* as it stands today it reads very much like an exposition of utilitarian philosophy, interspersed with disjointed dogmatic statements of the indispensability of the Nichiren Shō faith for the realization of the goal of human life, happiness.

The truth of the matter is that the basic faith of the Nichiren Shō Denomination—namely, that implicit faith in the Worship Object is sufficient to enable the individual believer to enter the state of buddhahood in his present existence—is dichotomous with utilitarian philosophy. The *Kachiron,* as edited, attempts to fuse these two basically antithetical teachings. It appears that Toda accomplished this fusion with a dual purpose in mind; first, because of his own personal blind devotion to Makiguchi, the *Sensei,* he was determined to make him immortal through his teachings (as he swore in his "prison vow"); and second, he saw an opportunity to establish Makiguchi as a martyr for the faith and thus provide the dynamic for renewed fervor of the group which had been begun before the war.

Pure textual criticism reveals the hand of the redactor, as, for instance, the anachronism of a reference to the atomic bomb (Makiguchi having died in prison during the Second World War).

Critics have pointed out errors in the transliterations of names of Western philosophers which occur in the text. However, the basic weakness or inconsistency of the work, as stated above, is in the attempt of the editor to fuse the basically humanistic philosophy of utilitarianism with belief in the teachings of the Nichiren Shō Denomination. To the Sōka Gakkai believer, though, this is not an inconsistency at all, but a logical development of the basic argument of the book. For him the utilitarian philosophy behind *Kachiron* has found its ultimate fulfillment in the "Orthodox" faith of Nichiren.

The Faith of Sōka Gakkai

The theoretical basis of Sōka Gakkai has been shown to be the philosophy of utilitarianism as developed by Makiguchi in his book *Kachiron*. The doctrinal home of the society is located in the 700-year-old tradition of Nichiren Buddhism as handed down through the Nichiren Shō Denomination as described in our chapter three. For the ordinary follower, however, much of this theory and doctrine is heavy going. With the masses converting to the faith, Toda and other leaders sensed early that the doctrine would have to be put into terms which the common man could grasp. Certain religious and cultural constants in the Japanese heritage could not be slighted if the masses were to be won. Worship of ancestors, for example, though in absolute contradiction to the basic faith of Nichiren Shō Buddhism, has such a strong hold on the average Japanese that even Sōka Gakkai has begun to make concessions.[6] Traditional Buddhist worship patterns, family altars, memorial services for the dead, pilgrimages to the head temple—these were all so much a part of the religious habits of the masses and of the Nichiren Shō Denomination itself (before its revival) that Sōka Gakkai found its expedient to utilize these traditions rather than to break with them.

The average follower is not expected to go too deeply into a study of doctrine, at least not on his own. Upon seeing my collection of books in Japanese on their teachings, one member of the society remarked, "How were you able to get your hands on these books? I have already reached the second stage in my preparation to be a lecturer and still haven't been given some of these books." In the question-answer period after one of Toda's public lectures a woman complained because she hadn't been able to win anyone to the faith. She said that she had gone to a local leader and he had told her that first of all she should attain the mind of Buddha (*busshin*) before she could hope to be able to win others. On hearing this the woman had jubilantly returned home, but then she realized that she didn't know what the mind of Buddha is. Consequently she asked Toda to explain it, but he only told her, with tongue in cheek, that when she had reached this state she would be in a class above Prime Minister Kishi. Yet, even if he did control the doses of doctrine the ordinary follower was to take, Toda himself knew the importance of grasping the teaching. He was an educator as well as an organizer. It was Toda's calling as an educator which attracted him to his revered *Sensei,* Makiguchi, and it was, no doubt, his talent as an organizer which attracted Makiguchi to Toda.

Within the limitations of the group's own concentrated purpose and stipulated goals, the individual follower is thoroughly indoctrinated and trained. In fact, Sōka Gakkai is conducting the most amazing program of indoctrination Japan has ever seen. It is difficult to conceive of a more thorough system of indoctrination of the laity by a religious group than Sōka Gakkai is achieving among its followers today. A convert begins his training by attending local lecture meetings where he is introduced to the scriptures (*Gosho*) and the indispensable manual (*Shakubuku Kyōten*). Right away he subscribes to the weekly and monthly periodicals, and begins to attend monthly or bi-monthly area lecture meetings as well as the regular meetings held in his own community. Later he is introduced to Toda's commentaries on the *Lotus Sūtra* (covering only chapters 2 and 16). Once a year the education department gives examinations and awards students with the four successive ranks of Associate Lecturer, Lecturer, Associate Teacher, or Teacher. Every member is expected to take the exams. In a study-conscious society and examination-oriented national system of education, Sōka Gakkai's indoctrination program is manifestly compatible with the climate.

What then are the teachings that every follower of this group must know? They can be described under the following headings: a shibboleth, a set of patent doctrines, and a simplified way.

The Shibboleth

"Any man can achieve happiness now." Each element of this statement has significance. Together these words constitute a proclamation which is not only designed to appeal to the masses living in the spiritual vacuum of postwar Japan, but is also cleverly aligned with the utilitarian philosophy of the *Kachiron* and the writings of Nichiren.

Happiness is the key word. It has universal appeal. It is not fair to say that in Sōka Gakkai the word has no spiritual content, but to the ordinary member it is closely enmeshed with worldly connotations. The average follower is not taught to redefine the word "happiness" in line with his new spiritual understanding; rather, he is led to believe that he has within his reach a tool to help him realize the happiness (defined by his own unaltered worldly standard) which had previously eluded him. The "reward of first belief," the cumulative merit resulting from activity of *shakubuku,* the efficacious merit of reciting for self and for others the prayer, *Namu Myōhōrengekyō*—all of these promises are held out as means of escape from specific misfortune such as sickness, failure in business, and loneliness. The cause of misfortune (synonomous with unhappiness) is false belief, either on the part of the individual in his present existence or through the cause-effect relationship inherited from some previous existence. To break the evil curse one simple incantation of the prayer is sufficient. Successive repetitions bring successive release, cumulative merit, and happiness.

Achievement of happiness as a human possibility is a central teaching which is best explained in the *Kachiron,* but the teaching is made more palatable to the average follower by the paraphrase in chapter 4 of the *Shakubuku Kyōten.* To quote a paragraph (in translation):

> When one says happiness, first he thinks of material or spiritual happiness. Frequently you hear, "I am not blessed

with material things but I am spiritually blessed, so I am happy, etc." It is not an overstatement, however, to say that no matter whether it be one of the world's "systems" or one of the "isms"—all are incapable of achieving the happiness which is the objective of human life. The more science progresses the greater the benefits it brings to human life. There are those who think that as science advances man will be able to live a life of greater happiness. Such people know neither science nor true religion. To explain this in simple terms: as over against science which investigates the outside world from the point of view of self, religion is the investigation and the solution to the problem of man's internal life. Therefore, no matter how much science advances and contributes to unlimited benefits and conveniences in all areas of life, it cannot solve the problem of the suffering which comes from childlessness, sickness of father, mother, wife, or child, an unhappy home, etc. Nor can it solve the sufferings which rise from anger, envy, covetousness, etc. Such sufferings cannot be healed by some sedative medicine. Religion alone can solve the question of the meaning of this life we are now living.

. . . by belief in this great religion we harmonize the rhythm of life with the rhythm of the universe and experience a complete feeling of living happiness. The great joy of life is itself the fountain-source of happiness.

Man can create values; in this lies man's greatness. All values are relative to their appropriated benefit to man. The goal of life is to achieve personal happiness. But, in order to realize the goal of human life, man must choose the correct path. This path is the Nichiren Shō faith. For, as Nichiren explained in the *Kaimokushō* (On Opening the Eyes), the root of all unhappiness is false belief. To achieve happiness and break the curse of false belief, man must turn to the truth in the *Lotus Sūtra,* the meaning of which is believed to have been fully discovered and preached by Nichiren alone. This truth can be summed up in one simple prayer of praise, referred to as the *daimoku: Namu Myōhōren-gekyō* (Hail to the Wonderful Truth of the *Lotus Sūtra*). Thus man can achieve happiness.

Any man is the target of the Sōka Gakkai advance. Though a good case could be made that this movement is nationalistic, Sōka Gakkai has openly announced its self-appointed mission to convert the world to the "true" faith. No man is lost. According to the teaching of the *Lotus Sūtra,* as interpreted by Nichiren, every man can attain buddhahood. This is the truth written "beneath the letter" of the *Lotus Sūtra.* Until the giving of this *sūtra* all belonging to "the world of those who hear the teaching" and "the world of those who are conscious of the external cause which is capable of developing the dormant seed of the Buddha mind within them"—all these people were considered to be lost because they were already self-satisfied and felt no need of salvation. But with the giving of the *Lotus Sūtra* it was made clear that these people too could attain buddhahood.

There is no reason why any man should be unhappy. This is the recurrent theme of the *shakubuku* teams bent on converting others to their faith. If you argue that you are already happy, they point out the insecurity of human existence, the uncertainty of the future, the possible calamities that may be just around the corner. If you say that you must be faithful to the religion of your parents, the strongest emotional religious tie for the ordinary Japanese, they point out that anyone should know that one's parents and ancestors above everything else want their children to be happy. If a person achieves the greatest happiness by converting to the Nichiren Shō faith, they argue, surely the parents and ancestors, no matter what their religion may have been, will look down upon them from the other world and smile because they are glad their children have found true happiness.

"Any man" evidently includes the Christian missionary. In a conference with Shirotake Watanabe, then student department chief, and Kazuya Morita, executive secretary, at the Sōka Gakkai Headquarters in Tokyo I was told that Christians are concerned only with ideas. "You think you can build your life on ideas," Morita warned. "But you cannot receive happiness except through the Great Holy One, Nichiren." Watanabe compared Christians to railroad engineers who knew all about the train but never hopped on board. "That's why you never reach the destination—happiness." Concluding the interview Morita advised, "If you taste the tea you will know its flavor."

Now is the time of salvation, according to Sōka Gakkai.

According to the teaching of Nichiren the spread of the Buddhist Dharma takes place in three stages: the period of the Upright Dharma *(shōhō)* which extended for a thousand years after the manifestation of the incarnate Buddha Gautama; the period of the Simulated Dharma *(zōhō)* which extended for the next thousand years and was characterized by the accommodated teaching; and the period of the End of the Dharma *(mappō),* the period when man was believed to be hopeless because he was left without the Dharma, which began in A.D. 1052 and is to extend for 10,000 years (interpreted to mean an indefinite period of time). This period of the End of the Dharma is marked by the appearance of the true follower of the *Lotus Sūtra* predicted in the *sūtra* and identified as Jōgyō Bosatsu (in Sanskrit: *Bodhisattva Vishista-caritra*), whose incarnation Nichiren is believed to have been. It is in this time when "false religions" flourish and the True Dharma has been forgotten that the "true follower of the *Lotus Sūtra*" (Nichiren) arises to call men back to the right path.

The current aggressive movement to propagate the faith gets its impetus from this emphasis on the importance of the *now,* for it is the belief of Sōka Gakkai followers that it is now that man can be saved, and it is now that man must be saved. To explain why the present twentieth century (and not the thirteenth century when Nichiren lived) is the time for the dissemination of the doctrine throughout the world, Sōka Gakkai claims that the sign which indicates the day has come for the world propagation of their faith is the tooth left at Taisekiji by Nikkō. The flesh adhering to this tooth began to grow and, when it was revealed in 1959, was seen to have completed the circumference. This is the sign that *now* is the time to win the world to Nichiren, the Real Buddha for this age.

A Set of Patent Doctrines

The teachings of the Nichiren Shō Denomination can become very complex for the initiated, if they probe into such traditional Mahāyāna concepts as *ichinensanzen* or the three bodies of Buddha; but for the members of Sōka Gakkai three basic doctrines found in Nichiren's writings and supplemented by six other derivative doctrines, are regarded as sufficient. The three basic doctrines are set forth in two of Nichiren's most significant works already briefly mentioned: *Kaimokushō* (On Opening of the Eyes) and *Kanjin Honzonshō* (On the Contemplation of the True Worship Object). In Nichiren Shō these teachings are referred to as (1) "The Five Sets of Comparisons," (2) "The Five Sets of Three Steps," and (3) "The Four Fates."

(1) "The Five Sets of Comparisons" is a good example of Nichiren's methodical study and comparison of the Buddhist *sūtras* throughout Buddhist history. Beginning his search for the true doctrine at the age of twelve and studying various Buddhist denominations in Japan, Nichiren finally reached the conclusion that the teachings of Tendai Daishi pointed to the real truth. His "comparisons" draw heavily upon Tendai's analysis of the Buddhist *sūtras.*

In comparing religious faiths Nichiren proceeded from the broad to minute distinctions, showing first that Buddhism is superior to all other religions, that Mahāyāna Buddhism is superior to Hīnayāna, the "true" doctrine of the *Lotus Sūtra* to the accommodated doctrine of all other *sūtras,* the last half of the *Lotus Sūtra* to the first half, and finally that the hidden truth beneath the written letter of the *Lotus Sūtra*—that is, the truth that the Buddha existed from eternity—is superior to the literal teaching of the *sūtra.*

(2) "The Five Sets of Three Steps" most plainly shows Nichiren's indebtedness to Tendai. Tendai Daishi's purpose had been to harmonize the *sūtras* so that obvious contradictions would be resolved and none of the *sūtras* slighted. Nichiren, however, perverted this original purpose and carried Tendai's classification through to a climax in the *Lotus Sūtra,* not as the most important *sūtra,* as Tendai taught, but as the only *sūtra* of relevance to man living in the period of the End of the Dharma. Then from this *sūtra* Nichiren further focused attention on the magic prayer, *Namu Myōhōrengekyō,* which he claimed contained the heart of the doctrine, adequate in itself alone to bring salvation to all mankind.

Nichiren, following Tendai Daishi, considered all extant *sūtras* to have been given by the historical Buddha himself. The first period of the "Five Sets of Three Steps," therefore, was the period of the lifetime of Gautama in which all of the *sūtras* were given. Then, in spite of obvious contradictions and inconsistencies, these numerous *sūtras* were said to represent one teaching in three stages or steps. The "text" of this teaching is to be found in the *Lotus Sūtra*, enlarged to include the *Sūtra on the Meaning of Infinity (Muryōgikyō)*, and the *Sūtra on the View of Fugen's Practice (Kan Fugenkyō)*. The "conclusion" is the *Nirvāna Sūtra (Nehangyō)*. All other *sūtras* make up the "introduction."

Thus, the first set of "three steps" is the first period of the giving of the *sūtras* divided into the three steps of "introduction," "text," and "conclusion." The second, third, fourth, and fifth periods are likewise broken down into three steps each, under the headings "introduction," "text," and "conclusion." In each new period the one teaching is narrowed down more until the "text" of the final period is stated simply as *Namu Myōhōrengekyō*, which, as has been said, is the kernel of Buddha's teaching.

(3) "The Four Fates" in the *Kanjin Honzonshō* describes the "rise and fall," that is, the fate (or career) of all teachings, and shows how Nichiren's own teaching had arisen to surpass all others. Thus, (a) Buddhism arises to replace all former alien religions, which fall into disuse; (b) the doctrine of the *Lotus Sūtra* then rises and all other Buddhist doctrines fade away; next, (c) the hidden teaching of the *Lotus Sūtra* concerning the primordial Buddha arises to displace all other interpretations of the *Lotus Sūtra;* and finally, (d) the teaching of Nichiren himself in the *Kanjin Honzonshō* arises as the final, supreme faith.

In addition to these three basic doctrines the Nichiren Shō Denomination has officially subscribed to six others, making a total of nine fundamental doctrines of the faith.

To summarize these doctrines, as Toda often did for the ordinary follower, they teach that the time has now come for the realization of the truth revealed by Nichiren; that is, that every man can attain buddhahood as he is in his present life, that Japan is the place, and that the simple prayer, *Namu Myōhōrengekyō*, is the means for achieving buddhahood and, hence, happiness.

The Simplified Way

For the ordinary Sōka Gakkai member there is a simplified way which is to be found in the practice of daily devotions and the acceptance of some distilled "teachings," which may be grouped under the general concept of "Rewards and Punishments." The average believer's faith is most often a composite of a few patent answers given by the leaders to answer his personal life-questions. Here are some of the questions, with the answers which Sōka Gakkai gives:

1. About Sickness. If you enter Sōka Gakkai and really believe, physical illness, whatever it may be, will be healed. The Great Holy One, Nichiren, in his reply to a priest, Ōta, listed six kinds of sickness. Of these, some, such as those caused from overeating or overdrinking, he said, could be healed by a physician or medicine; but some could be healed only by the Worship Object. The members of Sōka Gakkai are encouraged to use doctors, or any reasonable remedies, while at the same time relying on faith in the Worship Object. If a believer prays to the Worship Object while undergoing medical treatment, the cure will be more rapid and more complete. But to be saved from sickness caused by one's evil karma, only faith in the magical power of the Worship Object can avail.

2. About Death. All men one day must die; but for one who puts his faith in the Worship Object the day of death can be postponed for weeks or months, even years. The day of death can be postponed until the believer has had time to accumulate merit through the forced conversion of others, until he has had time to win his family and friends to the truth, to settle his financial accounts, or to attain the mind of Buddha so that in death he will attain the likeness (in physical countenance) of a buddha. Proof that one has died in the state of buddhahood (as related in a previous chapter) is seen in the condition of the corpse. There is a vague expectation of personal immortality in a life which extends beyond the grave, but only for those who have broken the chain of karma. For the less fortunate there awaits the grim prospect of endless rebirths, sometimes into lower forms of existence.

3. About Karma. As in other forms of Japanese Buddhism, belief in karma is held by followers of the Nichiren Shō Denomination. One's condition in this present existence is believed to be directly related to his deeds in a former existence, and this chain of cause and effect is believed to continue in an endless cycle. Fear of rebirth into a lower state of existence, as a beast or as a hungry demon of the nether world, is a very real motivation toward religious faith for many Japanese. Nichiren taught that the cycle of cause and effect could be cut and that man could break loose from his karma in order to attain the state of buddhahood through a realization of the truth (that the buddha-world exists and may be realized in man's present existence) revealed to man in the *Lotus Sūtra*.

4. About Suffering. In the teaching of Nichiren and Sōka Gakkai, human misery is the direct result of false belief. This false belief may be of the present or of some past existence, but through the law of cause and effect it is made to bear on the present. Human suffering can be alleviated only by right belief—that is, belief in the Worship Object of the Nichiren Shō Denomination. But there is meaning in suffering itself. Suffering is the mark of a human being, though this is not to be misinterpreted to mean that suffering is the result of human sin. Suffering produces the attitude of belief, and hence has meaning.

5. About the Purpose of Human Life. The utilitarian thought of Makiguchi's *Kachiron* concerning the creation of human values is widely disseminated among the believers. Unanimously they hold that man is born into this world to find happiness. Human life is the search for happiness. This happiness is interpreted in terms of the things which give individual, personal satisfaction: wealth, security, friends, family, health. Man is frustrated in his search for happiness by false belief. If he believes in the Worship Object he will begin to see proofs of the efficacy of this faith in terms of personal happiness. If the proofs are not soon forthcoming it is only because he does not truly believe.

For the believer who grasps the meaning of attaining the mind of Buddha there is no expectation of personal immortality or the continuation of the soul after the grave. To attain buddhahood is to realize the goal of no-self. For many, however, super-

stitious misunderstandings of the law of karma threaten them with
infinite rebirths as punishment for actions committed in the present
existence. Much of human suffering is attributed to this idea of
karma.

6. About Buddhahood. Toda interpreted the concept of becoming buddha *(jōbutsu)* in terms of man's temporal life. A
cheerful home, a secure, vigorous spirit, a business and home
life bubbling over with joy: this, taught Toda, is the state of
buddhahood. This he believed to be in keeping with Nichiren's
teaching that any man can become buddha in his present life.

The Worship of Sōka Gakkai Believers

At morning and evening worship before a paper replica of the
Great Worship Object which is enshrined in Taisekiji, the believer
intones selections from the *Lotus Sūtra,* bows humbly again and
again as he intones the sacred prayer, *Namu Myōhōrengekyō,*
and is content in his heart that he has found the "Way."

The believer looks upon his paper copy of the Great Worship
Object as a symbol of the presence of Nichiren in spirit and
power, but sometimes the symbol and the spirit are confused to
such an extent that the paper is considered to house a mysterious
magic. Untold misfortunes are expected to befall the person who
misuses or profanes the Worship Object. For many this piece of
paper on which is imprinted the sacred inscription of Nichiren,
whom they believe to be the Real Buddha, is in itself the essence
of Buddha.

Twice a day the Sōka Gakkai member is required to worship
before his family altar in which is enshrined his own personal
Worship Object. But neither the worship act nor the altar is
notably different from other Nichiren denominations.

The altar is simple and is marked by an absence of the color
or gaudiness which is characteristic of some Buddhist denominations in Japan. When the doors of the altar are opened the Worship Object is revealed as the central focus for the worship
service. The Worship Object sometimes is quite small, about
ten inches in length and about four inches wide, with black characters on a white background. In one altar I saw a quite large
reproduction with white letters on a black background.

On a shelf below the doors are placed a pair of candlesticks, a bowl with burning incense, a bowl of rice, and a cup of water. A pair of vases holds the evergreen branches of the Chinese anise (flowers are not used). The worshiper sits on his knees in Japanese fashion, facing the altar, holding a rosary in his two hands.

The act of worship consists of a lengthy (five to fifteen minutes) intonation of the prayer, *Namu Myōhōrengekyō,* just these words repeated over and over again in a chant. From time to time the incantation is broken to allow for a low bow of obeisance to the Worship Object and a quick rubbing of the prayer beads. Passionate prayer is often punctuated by a quickened tempo in rubbing the beads. When the occasion is a group meeting *(zadankai)* there is a leader who seats himself (or herself) immediately before the altar and the worshipers take their cues from him.

At a point about halfway through the worship service the leader begins to intone passages from the *Lotus Sūtra,* from either chapter 2 or chapter 16. Most of the worshipers follow these surprisingly long recitations from memory, but some of them read from abbreviated copies of the *Lotus Sūtra.* The service closes with another rather sustained period of chanting of the invocation.

In the *zadankai* (local group meeting), after this opening service of worship before the altar the group relaxes, men crossing legs, and the group leader takes charge. The meeting takes on the character of a "testimonial." The newest convert is called on to give his praise to the miraculous power of the Worship Object which he has personally experienced. Older members, though they have testified many times before, if there is a new face in the group will recount the miracles of their own healing or deliverance from financial difficulties. At a meeting the author attended, an old man brought out X-rays to prove to the "unbeliever" that his stomach ulcer had been cured. (He died in less than two months of stomach cancer.)

After these testimonies, a youth gets to his feet and leads the group in the rousing pep songs of the Sōka Gakkai youth department. A young girl follows, sometimes, going through the same gyrations as the boy. An old woman remarks, when a new song is introduced, "Let the young ones sing it; I guess I'm too old to learn."

Then the leader, trained through the program of the Sōka Gakkai education department, closes with a pep talk. For example, in explaining the meaning of the three "proofs"[7] of the validity of a religion—the "letter proof," the "reason proof," and the "actual proof"—a leader demonstrated the typical "logic" employed by Sōka Gakkai members to win converts. "If you have a cold, what do you do? You take cold medicine, don't you? We find out by reading the label ('letter proof') whether it is good for a cold or not. We decide then on the basis of our own reasoning ('reason proof') whether we think it is good or not. Then, if we take it and it works we know it is good medicine ('actual proof')." From this logic one is supposed to understand that only the Nichiren Shō faith is capable of saving man in this age of the End of the Dharma. For, says the leader, "You've got it now, haven't you? When you catch a cold you don't take worm medicine." With a big guffaw and a jab in the rib of the fellow squatting nearby on the mat floor, the members gathered at the zadankai had "got it," and were convinced that their religion had been "proven" once and for all to be the only true religion with power to save men in the present dispensation. They would try this example of the medicines the next time they went out to do shakubuku.

The leader continues, "There are many different kinds of rewards, but we have all received some wonderful reward from the Worship Object, haven't we? If there were no reward would there be five million families of believers? It's wonderful, isn't it? Wonderful to be a believer. We're all happy! All you folks who have found happiness through believing, raise your hands." Every hand is raised.

"Let's all believe! All around us people are saying all kinds of evil things about Sōka Gakkai. Don't let that bother you. Let's show them all that our faith is the only faith that can save Japan and the entire world." The group begins to leave, with a farewell to the hostess, and a final act of obeisance before the altar. Many would be walking home together, for most were nextdoor neighbors.

八章 A PILGRIMAGE TO THE FOOT OF MT. FUJI

The week beginning June 12, 1960, promised cloudy skies with the advent of the rainy season. But what was even more foreboding, a restlessness and throbbing resentment, carried through the arteries of the press to the nation and intensified by the scheduled visit of President Eisenhower, indicated that another kind of storm was in the offing.

It was no time to visit Mt. Fuji, but here I was, sprawled out over the narrow third class seat, and halfway across the aisle of the overnight "up-train" for Tokyo. Two hours before the train was due in Tokyo Station, with a small attaché case of clothing in one hand, a heavy briefcase of books in the other, a cumbersome umbrella stuffed under an arm, and uncombed hair stuffed under a straw hat, I detrained at Fuji Station.

From here I was to make a couple of transfers before reaching my goal, but connections were good and I found myself at the main gate of Taisekiji, the head temple of the Nichiren Shō Denomination, before eight o'clock.

Already we had met six crowded buses on the way, but there seemed to be no end to the crowd of visitors. When I arrived, there were some three or four hundred people waiting in line, in groups, under banners that read "Ōsaka District," etc. There was a man at a microphone giving instructions so that the crowd could board the buses with a minimum of confusion.

Everywhere young men wearing red armbands were running about discharging some responsibility. Later in the day a group of young men, about 200 in all, were singing the Sōka Gakkai theme song with gusto under the leadership of a young man who went through all the animations of a pep-squad leader. The expressions on some of the faces were as if their lives depended on this song and the way they sang it. Inside the main gate at the entrance of each of the twelve lodges which lined both sides of the path to the Worship Hall, two or more young men served as keeper-guides, each with a Sōka Gakkai badge in his lapel.

There were women with babies on their backs, bandaged and sickly people, old men and women. One woman was leading her blind husband; they stepped away from the crowd and she found a place for him to rest for a moment.

Everyone was orderly. There seemed to be no drinking or loud activity. Without exception everyone preparing to leave on the endless line of buses bowed first before the main gate. All showed deep respect for elders and those who were evidently teachers.

It was azalea time. Though earlier in the morning it had been almost cold, now the temperature was warming up and the clouds were lifting. Later in the day the top of Mt. Fuji, still snow-capped, was visible, floating on the clouds. Beside the long path azalea hedges were dazzling in their brilliance. The wide stone walk was bordered on both sides by a small artificial stream of water. Beyond this, symetrically on each side, were stone walls which enclosed the twelve lodges.

Topping the stone walls were the azalea hedges, some hanging luxuriantly down the sides, smaller plants gaining a toehold in crevices between the rocks of the wall. Purple azaleas made the red ones look orange.

There were pink azaleas and blue azaleas. And in the distance, throughout and surrounding the temple enclosure, huge, majestic cryptomeria trees lent an atmosphere of age and solemnity.

Finally I was introduced to the head of the student department of Sōka Gakkai, Mr. Watanabe. When I had stepped through the main gate I had noticed a tremor of uneasiness run through the crowd. I was a foreign intruder—evidently an outsider. Suitcases, umbrella, and straw hat—and, in addition, a "high nose" and "blue eyes." I was just as confused as they. I had written to the business office but had never received an answer. The temple was much larger than I had expected. In all this multitude of visitors I had no choice but to throw myself upon the mercy of the two men who came over to ask if I hadn't gotten off at the wrong bus stop or something. Eventually I made my purpose known and was guided to the temple headquarters of the Sōka Gakkai. After about an hour a young, clean-cut fellow (about 24) came to the gate where I had been waiting and asked me to come inside. I was led to the central building of this group—actually a small temple with altar. Here I was served tea and exchanged the formalities of introduction with Shirotaka Watanabe, student chief.

I told Watanabe frankly that I was a Christian and a missionary (something I hadn't mentioned to the various others who had questioned me), and that I had come to Taisekiji to get the answers to some of my questions. He was honest and frank. Why in the world had I come to the temple? Why hadn't I visited the headquarters of Sōka Gakkai in Tokyo where they were only too willing to answer any questions I had? I replied that I wasn't satisfied with some of the answers I had received from certain Sōka Gakkai members; I wanted to talk to the priests and religious scholars. These, I said, I expected to be able to find at the head temple.

Through Watanabe I gained entrance to the Great Lecture Hall and finally met Priest Jigaku Mizutani, the General Business Manager of Taisekiji. Mizutani and two other priests (one of whom was about 30 years old) met me in the conference room, which was decorated in excellent modern taste, with foam-rubber upholstered chairs. We exchanged introductions and Mizutani informed me that he had been expecting me. We were served tea. The atmosphere was friendly, and after I had once more carefully stated the purpose of my visit, Mizutani informed me that they were ready to help me to understand their faith to the best of their ability.

I noticed that each of the priests had entered the room carrying a small flat folder or book. I never managed to see what it contained. The priests were dressed in the plain white denim robes of their faith. The overgarment was of beautiful undyed silk.

I had three specific questions in mind and hoped that the conversation would proceed from there. The first question was:

(1) Do you respect or worship Gautama? The answer was "No." When I ventured to compare Gautama with Dainichi and

Amida I was told that he was of an entirely different nature. "Nichiren is held to be the one and only Buddha who has any relationship or saving power for us who live in the days of the End of the Law."

(2) What is your attitude toward Toda? The answer was that he was considered to be the greatest among the laymen. Upon his death he was given the title-rank of *Hokke Kōsō Kōtō* (Chief of all the Preachers of the *Lotus Sūtra*).

(3) What is your attitude toward the *Kachiron?* The priests said that they do not usually study this book in the course of their preparation. It is recommended to the layman to read, especially to the scholastic-minded, as a first step on the way to faith.

The priests explained many of their basic doctrines to me. There are three ways of leading men, they told me: by establishing the contact, by examples and illustrations, and by the preaching of the Dharma itself. Hence the priests recognize a gradual climbing of the ladder of faith. When questioned, however, they said that there are no ranks among those who have attained buddhahood.

In the course of the conversation the priests told me various details of religious services and activities of the Taisekiji. The ceremony for the accession of a new abbot upon the death of his predecessor (called *Daigawari*) was conducted on November 17, 1959, and Nittatsu Shōnin (age 58) became the 66th abbot in the direct succession from Nichiren. At this time the tooth of Nichiren with flesh growing on it and other treasures were shown to the believers. At no other time are these treasures exhibited.

Each year on April 7 there is a sort of housecleaning service at which they display the Imperial Worship Object (called the *Shishin gohonzo*n) which Nichiren prepared especially for the Emperor and his family when they shall have been converted to the true faith.

The temple ceremony which marks a new believer's entrance into the faith is called the "reception of the precepts" *(gojukai).* This, I was informed, corresponds to Christian baptism. The Worship Object is received on top of the head, and a replica of the Great Worship Object is presented to the initiate to become the central object of worship of his home.

I was shown the "Bible" of the faith, called the *Gosho* (Holy Writings), and was told that within these scriptures the five books of chief importance are the *Risshō Ankokuron,* the *Kaimokushō,* the *Kanjin Honzonshō,* the *Senjishō,* and the *Hōonshō.* These five are also referred to as the *Namu Myōhōrengekyō.* I expressed surprise that these should be equated with the sacred prayer which is the distinguishing mark of this faith. The answer was that it is this prayer which contains the essence of all the writings and ministry of Nichiren, and it is this prayer which contains the meaning of the *Lotus Sūtra,* which in turn contains all the meaning of all Buddhist *sūtras.*

The conversation shifted then to the subject of the exclusiveness of the Nichiren Shō Denomination, and I asked if the priest would help me to distinguish between it and the Nichiren Denomination. One of the priests supplied me with this simple comparison. In the Nichiren Denomination the Buddha is Gautama; the Dharma is the *Namu Myōhōrengekyō* of the letter of the *Lotus Sūtra;* and the priest is Nichiren. In the Nichiren Shō Denomination the Buddha is The Holy One, Nichiren; the Dharma is the *Namu Myōhōrengekyō* of the Three Great Hidden Laws; and the priest is Nikkō. It was requested that if I ever wrote anything for publication on the Nichiren Shō Denomination that I remember above all else that the faith centers in "The great true object of worship of the altar of the basic doctrine of the Great Holy One, Nichiren"; in other words, the treasured Great Worship Object kept at Taisekiji.

Before the conference ended I was able to ask a few incidental questions on obscure points which were not covered in the dictionaries, and also to make some miscellaneous queries. For example: What about the "merit of first belief" *(shoshin no kudoku)*? The priests said that such merits are definitely recognized, but that these were small merits and that the great merit may not be realized immediately. What about karma? Aren't there some karma effects that no amount of faith will erase? Yes, but the effects of karma may be minimized and weakened. Furthermore, there is hope for the final elimination of the effects of evil karma in future lives.

I was not able to stay in the lodgings of the temple because I was a non-believer. Mizutani was very helpful, however, and secured for me an upstairs room in an inn operated by a Sōka Gakkai member, just at the entrance of the temple grounds, where I stayed for several days. From two walls of sliding glass panels I could look full face upon the main gate where everyone arrived and from which everyone boarded the buses. I could see their first and last acts of worship. *Nammyōhōrengekyō, Nammyōhōrengekyō, Nammyōhōrengeykō,* the prayer sounded as they intoned the chant three times in sonorous tones standing before the gate facing toward the Main Hall, the original worship hall. The chant was followed by a brief rubbing of the prayer beads between the palms of the hands, then a bow (sometimes twice).

From the window I watched the pilgrims as they lined up preparing to board the buses. Everyone seemed to be carrying a small bundle of green leaves. Later I discovered that these were leaves of the Chinese anise (or magnolia) which is the only "flower" used to decorate the altar of this faith. Little stands temporarily erected about the temple outskirts sold the leaves along with books and other supplies for study and worship.

The main gate had recently been painted a brilliant lacquer red. It apeared to be about eight stories in height. Measuring I could count 12 *ken,* which means that it is 72 feet wide. My host later verified my calculations and said that it is the second largest wooden temple gate in Japan.

The various groups under their banners, lined up in front of this gate waiting to board the buses, represented various districts throughout Japan. Each district is appointed a time to come during the visiting days, from Saturday to Monday. For example, the first week of each month is designated for the Kansai district, etc. Worshipers come in groups, for the sake of economy (it costs each member yen 250 for a night's lodging, including meals— though they bring their own rice—about 75¢) as well as for efficiency in handling them. The purpose of these visits to Taisekiji is to worship the Great Worship Object, which is revealed to the believers at a special service of worship. During their two-day visit there are various discussion meetings, an evening lecture on the scriptures, held in the big auditorium, seating capacity 5,000.

But since my visit the crowds have increased and a new worship hall, the Grand Reception Hall, with a seating capacity of 15,000, has been constructed. Some of the pilgrims enjoy sightseeing in the foothills of Mt. Fuji. And, of course, all pay their respects to Toda's grave.

The endless line of pilgrims! Endless! Until 12:00 o'clock noon I hardly saw a break in it. After lunch, however, I noticed that the crowd seemed to be decreasing. According to my host they would all be gone by evening. By 1:00 p.m., sure enough, there was no one waiting before the main gate, and workmen and women were already beginning to sweep the walks and sprinkle water to settle the dust.

I took a walk up to the pagoda. Even before I had time to take in the exquisite beauty of the five-roof building itself, guarded on all sides by giant cryptomeria, the bushwarbler called from a pine thicket and I was entranced. I thought, can the mockingbird back home sing like this? There at the pagoda was Toda's grave. The urn to hold burning incense had already cracked because of the heat of the many, constant prayer offerings, and a new open urn had been provided.

At 2:00 o'clock I was walking along the path, returning to my quarters, when I heard the chant of many voices, intoning the familiar *Namu Myōhōrengekyō* over and over again. A bell rang —a call to prayer. From the Guest Hall priests began to descend and hastily form a line. One younger fellow was late. Later I learned that this was a special service in the Worship Hall where the Great Worship Object is kept, especially for the leaders of Sōka Gakkai who had remained to clean up after the main crowd had returned.

Along the azalea-lined path there were entrances to guest houses (dormitories) with such names as Rentō-bō, Honjū-bō, etc. The ending -*bō* means "room" or "temple." In this case it refers to a lodging place within the temple precincts. There are six of these guest houses on each side of the walk, the largest one accommodating 450 guests. A priest is in charge of each and lives here with his wife and family. Mizutani, I learned, besides being business manager, is in charge of the Hyakkan-bō (No. 4).

Toward evening the gate turns back into a typical Japanese
temple entrance. The luster fades, the loving hands rubbing rosaries
having returned to the cities. Now country children use the
majestic structure as a backstop for their softball games, or hide
the thimble up behind the sacred name plaque. A man and his wife
going home from work cross the threshold without so much as a
bow.

Suppertime, and all is deserted. Mt. Fuji floats silently in a
white mist. I wrote down a few reflections in my diary.

It has been a long, long time since I've thought so seriously
and earnestly about my own faith. Here to study Buddhism,
engrossed daily in difficult reading and conversations on the
Nichiren Shō faith, still my mind constantly reverts to my
own faith and the faith of my own people. Is Christianity after
all just this: the faith of my own people? These Nichiren followers are so full of love for their own country and its traditions. They are so proud of Nichiren. They are trying so
hard to convince themselves that he was and is the eternal,
primordial Buddha. Is the fire and fever of religion found in
following a man who believes? How important man is! I
couldn't help bowing before Toda's tomb, out of respect for a
dedicated man. My Christian faith not satisfied, I prayed that
all his followers would transfer their loyalty to Christ. But are
Japanese so different from us? These Sōka Gakkai people are
loyal to a man—to Toda. Now it is the memory of the man
that fills them. With Toda it was the memory of Makiguchi
who died for his beliefs in prison. But what were Makiguchi's
beliefs? It was Toda who had to make the transfer and the
interpolation in terms of Nichiren Buddhism. Always the immediate, living teacher wins our loyalty. What will happen to
the Sōka Gakkai now? Can these people transfer their loyalty
to the young Ikeda? As Thomas Mann so clearly pointed out
in his Joseph series, it is the first of the four patriarchs who
has the real inspiration, the second solidifies and crystallizes
the teaching. But is Ikeda to prove to be the third generation
Jacob, the usurper? In the graveyard behind the original

Worship Hall lie the ashes of 65 patriarchs from Nichiren and Nikkō down to Nichijun. It has always been a man who stood for the Buddha. Is Christ no more than this? Do I have infinitely more than they because I set my sights on Christ? If Christ is all that he is but not God, is he better for me than Nichiren is for them? What has become of my early passion to follow Christ? Could a human like Toda pull more from me? Could I bow my head to a contemporary man? Would I be able to follow him implicitly as they follow Toda? Would I lose by trying to be like him? Or, as with Sōka Gakkai followers, could I ever be content with merely following his orders blindly? When there is no man whom they can respect like Toda to give the marching command, what will they do? Why, O why, didn't more Japanese Christians die for Christ in prison during the war, as Makiguchi died for his faith? Would that have been too much to ask of them? Here is something that we Christians in Japan today must face every day of our lives. How can we who have loyalty to one—Christ— divide this loyalty, even for form's sake? Much more, how can we recant; how can we deny Him under persecution? Isn't there anything greater than the exigency of the moment?

June 13, 1960 (Monday)
at Taisekiji, Fujinomiya

On Monday evening after supper my host guided me through the temple grounds and showed me the various buildings. An old gate, the original one, led to the temple enclosure. The main gate, which was visible from my window, was built in 1713 under the auspices of Tennei'in, wife of the 6th Tokugawa *shōgun,* Ienobu. Farther along the path there was another, much smaller gate, called the *Nitenmon,* a truly lovely wooden structure. Passing through this gate we saw, on our left, a small building which houses a large drum, and opposite it on the right another which houses the temple bell. Immediately ahead, the goal to which the path leads, was the main hall which was then being painted and repaired. This hall was constructed in 1629 at the time of the 18th patriarch, Nissei, under the auspices of the wife of the Lord of

Awa. From a glance I gained through the door and from pictures which have appeared in the organization's publications, the interior of this hall must be very much like the one described by Lloyd in *The Creed of Half Japan:*

> . . . there is an absolute *stūpa* or tabernacle, such as we found in the ancient *chaityas* in India, and symbolical of the *stūpa* which descended from heaven in chap. xiv of the "Saddharma-pundarika." In front of this tabernacle is the usual "table of prothesis" which is to be found in all Buddhist temples in Japan, and in front of that, again, what may be called the Choir, with the desks for the monks. Over this part, which comes about the middle of the building, is a baldacchino or umbrella from which hang strings of flowers in thin brass, the whole being intended to symbolize the "Pentecostal" shower of celestial flowers with which the action of the "Saddharma-pundarika" commences.[1]

In this main hall the Great Holy One, Nichiren, is the Worship Object, and it was here that the installation of St. Nittatsu as abbot was announced to Nichiren in November, 1959.

Returning in the direction of the main gate, after we had passed through the Nitenmon we took the path to the right which led through a large, new gate. This opened on a modern, ferro-concrete, six-story lecture hall, a very impressive building, which is a monument to the enthusiasm and administrative skill of the Sōka Gakkai. The building was dedicated on March 1, 1958, and a total number of 210,000 believers are reported to have made the pilgrimage to celebrate the event. Nearby a smaller, extremely modern concrete building, a recreation hall (as it is designated) containing 1,000 mats (one mat measuring 3 ft. by 6 ft.), was also contributed by Sōka Gakkai.

The original Grand Reception Hall at Taisekiji was destroyed by fire during the Second World War because of the carelessness of Japanese troops stationed there. At the time of the visit being described here (1960) a temporary structure was standing on the site, but now a new ferro-concrete, five-story structure, completed on March 2, 1964, and dedicated on April 1, has risen from the ruins. When the campaign for raising funds for this building was launched (in 1960) the goal was yen 1 billion (approximately $3 million). In a few days, Sōka Gakkai reports, three times this amount had been subscribed. The building required 158,313 man days, or 1,484,649 man hours, taking two years for completion. Materials were imported from all over the world: stones from numerous countries, cedar from Canada, and marble from Italy. The shell-shaped roof is reported to weigh 10,000 tons, set in special ball-bearing supports to give exceptional resistance to earthquakes. Through the main entrance to the building 5,000 people can go and come at one time. The main floor waiting room alone will accommodate 3,000. In the front wall of the entrance to the second floor, where worship is paid by the masses to the Great Worship Object, a magnificent mural of the mythical phoenix is set. The entire area of the building covers 4,584 square meters with a floor space of 10,455 square meters. The height is 25 meters (82 feet). Chandeliers for the main worship hall were imported from Europe, and the cypress of the ceiling was imported from Taiwan.

Traditionally the "holy of holies" has been the Worship Hall (called the *Hōanden*) where the Great Worship Object, the sacred writing of Nichiren, was enshrined at the time of my visit. This Worship Object, the quintessence of the faith, is a black lacquered camphor wood plaque, 144 by 65 centimeters in size, on which Nichiren himself is said to have written the epitome of his insight into Buddhist truth—the culmination of all that he taught. In technical terms, the Worship Object is a *mandala*. The root meaning of the Sanskrit term *mandala* is "circle," and this term was used to describe the basic concept governing the relations of one king (in India) with another.[2] Mandalas have been used in Buddhism for a long time, especially in such esoteric sects as Shingon which has two Mandalas, the male and female, called respectively the *Vajra* and *Garbha* Mandalas. In the case of the Shingon Denomination the Mandala itself is a pictorial representation of the cosmos—a scroll on which are drawn numerous figures of buddhas and bodhisattvas. The Mandala written by Nichiren and enshrined here at Taisekiji does not consist of pictures but rather the *names* (in Chinese characters) of the entities depicted. The Nichiren Mandala (the Great Worship Object) is a symbolic representation by means of writing in Chinese characters the names of those who participated in the scene in the *Lotus Sūtra* where a great *stūpa* containing Tahō (in Sanskrit: *Prabhūta-ratna*), a former Buddha, descends from heaven and invites Gautama to enter as a reward for his wonderful teaching of the truth of the *Lotus Sūtra*. This is the scene symbolized by the architecture of the main hall at Taisekiji, already described. The words of the *daimoku,* the magic prayer which is the essence of Nichiren's teaching and the focus of the Nichiren faith, *Namu Myōhōrengekyō,* occupy a commanding central position and take up most of the plaque. The names, Shaka (Gautama) and Tahō, on either side of the *daimoku* are surrounded by the names of various bodhisattvas and spirits and demons that witnessed the event (as recorded in the *Lotus Sūtra*). According to Nichiren this Mandala contains the essence of the meaning of the Buddhist Dharma, the summary of the teaching of the *Lotus Sūtra,* and the key to man's salvation.

In our tour we passed the numerous residences where the priests live with their families, where guests are entertained overnight. Beyond the graveyard, across a concrete bridge (also built by Sōka Gakkai), up a long flight of granite steps, almost completely hidden from view in a grove of ancient cryptomeria, stands the truly magnificent five-roof pagoda, with the new tomb of Toda beside it. This pagoda was begun in 1713 at the same time as the main gate, built through the initiative of Tennei'in, wife of Ienobu, but it was not finished until the time of the 31st patriarch, Nichiin, through a gift of Katsusumi Itakura, Lord of Kameyama Castle. The pagoda faces west, the direction of India, for, as my host explained, just as the moon rises in the west and proceeds to the east, so Buddhism originated in India and came to Japan; but the sun rises in the east and proceeds to the west, symbolic of the true faith which arises in Japan and proceeds to India and the west. All other buildings face south.

After I had returned to my room my host came in for a chat. He was eager to have me resolve all my questions and doubts and become a devout believer as he and his wife are. He told me about himself. For ten years he had served in the police depart-

ment of Numazu. After this he spent eight years in China directing the inspection of wool, hemp, and cotton. After the war he
returned to his native home at the entrance of Taisekiji. He re-
members the temple as it was in the days before its current face-
lifting through the efforts of Sōka Gakkai. But he himself is now
a fervent Sōka Gakkai member. He told me of how he had been
a classmate of the present abbot for eight years. Priests are sent
to the temple at the age of eight and attend the public school
nearby. My host is convinced that the Nichiren Shō faith is the one,
true faith for the world. Over and over again he urged that no
other faith would satisfy. Only his faith gives true happiness, the
goal toward which all humanity is striving.

Together we looked at various books which I had brought
with me. I explained how far I had advanced in my study and
what the object of this research was. He shook his head in dis-
appointment when he realized that I was content with such a
superficial investigation. You will never understand until you believe, he repeated again and again. He went to his room to bring
back his scriptures, and we read from them together. Several
places he had marked, especially to help him win the non-believer.
He was always kind and considerate, eager to try to see my point
of view, but never yielding in his prime objective: to win me over.

One morning I awoke at 4:30 to the ringing of the temple
bell—a soft, musing tone—as if it were coming from some great
distance; unhurried, sustained—as if someone were standing beside the bell, meditating, and then, now and then, was inspired to
strike it a blow.

When I returned from my early morning walk my host was
in his room reading aloud from the scriptures, in the familiar
chant. Later in the day I returned to the inn and smelled incense
as I climbed the stairs. This time the voice I heard was that of the
wife. Was this her time of day to say prayers? Members are
taught to pray twice a day—morning and evening. Performing
these prayers is the first of the two obligations of a believer, and
is called *gongyō*. The other obligation which every believer must
assume is *shakubuku*.

In the afternoon Priest Mizutani guided me through the new

Great Lecture Hall. It is of very modern design, equipped with self-operating elevators, conference rooms exquisitely furnished, small assembly rooms with mat floors, and a large auditorium (also with mat floor) which accommodates from four to five thousand worshipers. (Chairs are never used on mat floors.) There is, in addition, an extensive roof garden (over the auditorium), and a classroom for priests who come in the summer for training sessions.

The head abbot, Nittatsu Shōnin, is young—at that time 58 years of age. Mizutani explained that it was good that he was so young and strong since his duties are strenuous. He has official duties in the middle of the night. From 1:00 to 3:00 o'clock a.m. his duty was "The Great Peace to the People." Other duties concern the offices of respect that must be paid to the various worship objects in different buildings. Just going from one to the other is ample exercise. Priests live ordinary lives, no different from the laymen. They shave their heads and wear a special white garment, but otherwise they marry, take three meals a day, smoke, drink—anything, as long as it is not to excess. (On my first evening trip with my host we had engaged in conversation one priest who had evidently overstepped the line of moderation with respect to drink.)

I noticed that very little mortar is used in the building structures. One priest whom we met explained that in this area of Japan the earth is not suitable for use as mortar because of lack of clay content, and that building materials have traditionally been confined to wood and metal, sometimes with thatch roofs. This condition is certainly attested to in the surrounding farm dwellings. But it is also characteristic of the older buildings of the temple itself. Though lack of mortar makes the general appearance of the buildings somewhat more prosaic than those of Kyōto or Nara, nevertheless, the copper roofs of the main gate and the Nitenmon, and the main hall, are works of fine craftsmanship.

The morning for my trip on to Tokyo came. I was to board the bus at 8:50. According to the train schedule, I should arrive in Tokyo at about 12:30 noon the same day. My host and I went together to purchase a few books which I hadn't seen before.

The wife was dressed in her best kimono; evidently she was going somewhere. I gathered, through overhearing the conversation, that she was going to visit a friend in town to try to convert her. We boarded the same bus. It was difficult to talk, for our bus took the bumpy, narrow shortcut to the Fujinomiya station, but I finally managed to ask her a leading question. I felt that I had to know the reason behind all this fervor for the faith. My question was, "Have you no children?" Then she told me about her daughter, who was a victim of spinal meningitis. Everything began to fit, like pieces of a puzzle. This was the girl I had seen one day, squatting in a corner of the bathing room, brushing her hair without looking in a mirror. She had looked at me out of the corner of her eye with the sheepish, frightened look of a cowed animal. I had taken her for an idiot, but hadn't yet established her relation to the keeper of the inn. This also explained the queer, animal-like sounds from the altar room when the mother was praying. Had this girl been trying to pray too? Was she made to pray? This was, without doubt, the suffering from which they were seeking deliverance, the burden that my host and his wife were learning to bear through the strength of their faith. Had they indeed found the answer? Did they wait daily upon the miracle?

NOTES AND ACKNOWLEDGMENTS

2. Religions of the Here and Now

1. *Asahi Shinbun* (Asahi News), July 6, 1957.

2. The most serious attempt at an accurate presentation of the statistics on new religions in Japan was that made by William P. Woodard, editor of *Contemporary Religions in Japan*, in issues of this periodical beginning in December, 1961. These figures may be compared with those of the Ministry of Education in December, 1966. Their individual findings are tabulated below:

	Woodard Dec. 31, 1958	Ministry of Education Statistics as of Dec. 31, 1966
Ananaikyō	85,350	216,341
Konkōkyō	605,572	543,389
Kurozumikyō	751,670	651,454
Ōmoto	103,482	136,454
P. L. Kyōdan	854,300	1,079,150
Reiyūkai Kyōdan	3,737,577	4,198,635
Risshō Kōseikai	1,415,663	2,505,728
Sekai Kyūseikyō	398,174	639,816
Sōka Gakkai	(4,000,000)	15,234,136
Tenrikyō	2,388,431	2,459,009
Seichō no Ie	1,533,624	1,457,778

3. See McFarland, H. Neill, "The New Religions of Japan," *Contemporary Religions in Japan*, I.3, 4 (September and December, 1960); Schiffer, Wilhelm, "New Religions in Postwar Japan," *Monumenta Nipponica*, XI.1, p. 1 ff., 1955, and Watanabe, Baiyū, "Modern Japanese Religions, Their Success Explained," *Monumenta Nipponica*, 1957, XIII.1-2, pp. 153 ff. For a recent clear listing of the characteristics which the popular sects have in common see Offner, Clark B., and Van Straelen, Henry, *Modern Japanese Religions* (Rupert Enderle, Tokyo, 1963, and Twayne Publishers, Inc., New York), pp. 28-40. Perhaps the best statement on the new religions in the Japanese language is Saki, Akio, *Shinkō Shūkyō* (New Religions) (Aoki Shoten, Tokyo, 1960).

4. Schiffer, Wilhelm, "New Religions in Postwar Japan," *Monumenta Nipponica*, XI.1. Here he lists the opinions of several recent scholars and sources.

5. Watanabe, Baiyū, "Modern Japanese Religions," *Monumenta Nipponica*, XIII.157.

6. *Ibid.*

7. James, William, *The Varieties of Religious Experience* (Longmans, Green, and Co., London and New York, 1902), p. 48.

8. Kobayashi, Sakae, "Ōmoto, a Religion of Salvation," *Japanese Religions*, II.1 (April, 1960), pp. 40-41.

9. Watanabe, *op. cit.*, pp. 154 ff.

10. Weber, Max, *The Protestant Ethic and the Spirit of Capitalism*, tr. Talcott Parsons (Charles Scribner's Sons, New York, 1930).

11. For a discussion of this traditional respect for authority (*nagai mono ni wa makarero*, "yield to those above you") in the Japanese social behavior see Stoetzel, *Without the Crysanthemum and the Sword* (a UNESCO Survey, New York, 1955).

12. See Nishio, Harry K., "Comparative Analysis of the Risshō Kōseikai and the Sōka Gakkai," *Asian Survey*, 7.11.776-790 (November, 1967), for the sociological implications of this appeal.

13. *The Sokagakkai* (published by the Seikyō Press, Tokyo, 1960), pp. 95-96.

14. See article in the *Asahi Shinbun* (Asahi News), Osaka, July 6, 1957, in which several scholars and writers were questioned concerning their opinions regarding the popularity of Sōka Gakkai.

15. See Alfred Bloom's interesting article, "Is the *Nembutsu* Magic?" *Japanese Religions*, I.3 (October, 1959), pp. 31-35.

16. *Seikyō Gurafu* (The Seikyo Graphic), November 26, 1964.

17. Kudō, Takuya, "The Faith of Sōka Gakkai," *Contemporary Religions in Japan*, II.2 (June, 1961), pp. 5-6.

18. *Kojiki-den*, Vol. I, quoted in D. C. Holtom, *The National Faith of Japan* (Kegan Paul, London, 1938), pp. 23-24.

19. Ōno, Sokyo, *The Kami Way* (International Institute for the Study of Religions, Tokyo, 1959), pp. 107-108.

20. *Shakubuku Kyōten* (Manual on Forced Conversions), Sōka Gakkai, 1951, p. 53.

21. Quoted by Kobayashi in his article, "The 'Peaceful Co-existence' of Intellectual and Magical Elements in Japan's New Religions," in *Japanese Religions*, I.4 (January, 1960), pp. 28-31.

22. Holtom, D. C., *op. cit.*, pp. 268-281.

23. Fujieda, Masakazu, "The Church of World Messianity," *Contemporary Religions in Japan*, I.4 (December, 1960), pp. 33-34.

24. Kobayashi, Sakae, "Shinshūkyō no Oshieru Mono" (What the New Religions Teach), in *Nippon ni Okeru Kirisutokyō to Shoshūkyō to no Sesshoku no Mondai* (The Contact of Christianity and Other Religions in Japan) (published by the United Church of Christ in Japan, 1960), pp. 155 ff.
25. *Ibid.*, pp. 111 ff.
26. *Cf.* Schneider, Delwyn B., *Konkōkyō: A Japanese Religion* (ISR Press, Tokyo, 1962).

3. Japan's Buddhist Prophet

1. Jackson, Herbert C., *Man Reaches Out to God* (The Judson Press, Valley Forge, Penna., 1963), p. 69.
2. From the *Tannishō*, appearing in English translation in de Bary, Wm. Theodore, *et al.*, *Sources of the Japanese Tradition* (Columbia University Press, New York, 1958), p. 217; see also pp. 209-210.
3. For an English translation see Lloyd, Arthur, *The Creed of Half Japan* (Smith Elder & Co., London, 1911), pp. 307 ff.
4. Nichiren, *Kaimokushō* (On Opening the Eyes), in the Toda edition, *Kaimokushō-ge*, published by Sōka Gakkai, 1953, p. 112.
5. These documents are quoted, with Nichiren's signature and date, in Nakamura, *Bukkyō Tehodoki* (Hosoi Seidō, Tokyo, 1959), pp. 138-139. See also *Shakubuku Kyōten*, p. 210. Kodaira in *Sōka Gakkai*, p. 29, quotes a writing of Nikkō, called *Nikkō Yūikai Okibumi*, dated January 13, 1334, which states that only the doctrine of Taisekiji is true to the teachings of Nichiren.
6. The other five disciples of Nichiren were: Nikō (1252-1314), who became Abbot of the Kuonji at Mt. Minobu; Nisshin (1258-1334), who followed Nikō as Abbot of Kuonji in the year 1313; Nichirō (1242-1320), who founded the Ikegami Branch of the Nichiren Denomination; Nitchō (1251-1317), who served at Mt. Mama (Chiba Prefecture) after the Sado exile until the death of his father, after which time he devoted himself to the service of his father's grave; Nisshō (1235-1323), a scholar who compiled Nichiren's writings, later left Minobu to seek converts in Kamakura.
7. Probably the literal meaning is intended here in sarcasm, but the phrase, *"Doko no uma no hone ka wakaranai"* (No one knows what horse's bones these are) means something like the equivalent of, "Who in the world is this fellow?"
8. These are listed in the statistics of William P. Woodard, *Contemporary Religions in Japan*, II.4 (December, 1961), pp. 63 ff.
9. *Shakubuku Kyōten* (Manual on Forced Conversions), edited

by Kodaira and published by the Sōka Gakkai Press, 1951, pp. 134-136. This classification is referred to in Japanese as the *goji hakkyō* (five periods, eight *sūtras*).

10. Nichiren, *Kaimokushō* (On Opening the Eyes), in the Toda edition, *Kaimokushō-jō* (published by the Sōka Gakkai, 1953), p. 95. Here the text of Nichiren's evaluation of the *Lotus Sūtra* appears. Toda's translation into modern Japanese is found on p. 97.

11. See Müller, F. Max, *The Sacred Books of the East,* (Clarendon Press, Oxford, 1884), Vol. XXI, Introduction, p. xxii.

12. The three periods of the Dharma, according to the Nichiren Shō Denomination, are these: The *Shōhō* (Upright Dharma) which began in 949 B.C., the date Nichiren accepted as the year of Gautama's death; the *Zōhō* (Imaged Dharma), beginning one thousand years after Gautama's death and extending for another thousand years; and the *Mappō* (End of the Dharma), the period of decadence which Nichiren claimed to have been ushered in by himself (in the 13th century) and which he predicted would extend for ten thousand years—or forever.

13. This is chapter 14 according to Kern (*The Saddharma Pundarīka,* Clarendon Press, Oxford, 1909), and is translated by him as "Issuing of Bodhisattvas from the Gaps of the Earth." It is chapter 15 in the text accepted by Nichiren Shō and is called in Japanese, *Jūchi-yuijutsuhon* or *Jūji-yuijutsuhon.*

14. Nichiren, *Kanjin Honzonshō* (On contemplation of the True Worship Object), Toda's edition (published by Sōka Gakkai, 1955). The text is found on pp. 267–268, giving Nichiren's explanation that the bodhisattvas headed by Jōgyō Bosatsu were entrusted with the spreading of the teaching of the *Lotus Sūtra.* (Toda's comments are found on p. 270.) Later, pp. 290–291, Nichiren explains that now is the time when the bodhisattvas are to be revealed. Toda, commenting on this, joins Jōgyō Bosatsu to Nichiren.

15. Nakamura, *Bukkyō Tehodoki,* p. 152.

16. The Four Noble Truths are: (1) Life is *suffering.* The human body, in common with all matter, is in a state of perpetual change and flux; it is impermanent and subject to suffering. (2) The origin of suffering is *craving,* born out of ignorance. The craving for pleasure, lust, sensuous delight in the things of this world—these experiences, if cherished and clung to, produce birth, and birth produces decay and death; i.e., the whole cycle of suffering. (3) The extinction of suffering depends upon forsaking, giving up, and *detaching* oneself from craving. Anyone who regards the

delights of this world as (a) impermanent, (b) painful, (c) without a permanent ego, overcomes this craving. (4) The way to the extinction of suffering is the *Noble Eightfold Path:* right understanding, right intention, right speech, right action, right living, right effort, right mindfulness, and right concentration.

17. Nakamura, *ibid.,* p. 159.

4. The Martyr and the Organizer

1. Kodaira, *Sōka Gakkai* (Shinpūsha, 1958), p. 77.
2. Woodard, W. P., "The Wartime Persecution of Nichiren Buddhism," *The Transactions of the Asiatic Society of Japan* (Tokyo, 1959), Third Series, VII, pp. 108 ff.
3. Kodaira, *op. cit.,* p. 84.
4. Saki, Akio, and Oguchi, Iichi, *Sōka Gakkai* (Aoki Shoten, Tokyo, 1957), p. 160.
5. Kodaira, *op. cit.,* pp. 84–85.
6. Kobayashi, Sakae, "*Sōka Gakkai,* a Strange Buddhist Sect," *Japan Christian Quarterly,* XXIV. 2 (April, 1958), p. 110.
7. *Shinshūkyō Shinbun* (The New Religions News), November 20, 1955.
8. The report appears as an appendix to *Nippon ni Okeru Kirisutokyō to Shoshūkyō to no Sesshoku no Mondai.*
9. Takase, Hiroi, *Daisanbunmei no Shūkyō* (Religion of the Third Civilization) (Kōbundō, Tokyo, 1962), pp. 123 ff.
10. *Seikyō Gurafu* (The Seikyo Graphic), Sōka Gakkai periodical, May, 1960.

5. The Smashing of Idols

1. The word kami, ordinarily used to designate Shintō deities, is defined in the *Shakubuku Kyōten* as the name of beings whose function it is to protect the followers of the true Buddhist Dharma. This idea of the function of the traditional Japanese deities is not new with Sōka Gakkai. By the end of the Heian period (ca. A.D. 1,100) a syncretic form of Shintō, called *Ryōbu Shintō,* had evolved which was especially related to esoteric Buddhism. Buddhist deities were assumed to be the real entities of the traditional Shintō deities which were only "reflections." Great Shintō deities such as the Sun Goddess (Amaterasu) were identified with particular buddhas or bodhisattvas, while lesser Shintō deities were assigned the role of "protector" of the devout, a role similar to that given to the deva gods in primitive Indian Buddhism. It was a reversal of this idea that was back of the "Badger Incident" described here.

2. Takase, *op. cit.,* p. 160.

3. Lloyd, *op cit.*, p. 322.
4. *Ibid.*, p. 310.
5. Nichiren, *Kanjin Honzon Tokuishō*, found in the *Gosho* (Holy Writings), p. 972.
6. Nichiren, *Kaimokushō* (On Opening the Eyes), Toda's edition, p. 63.
7. *Shakubuku Kyōten*, Part I, ch. 7, p. 152.
8. The attitude toward ancestor worship accounts, in part, for the slow progress of Sōka Gakkai in Okinawa, where worship of ancestors (*ihai sūhai*) is more entrenched today than it is in Japan. It will be noted that Sōka Gakkai and other Nichiren denominations were persecuted during World War II because of this antithetical stand on the issue of worship of ancestors (which includes emperor worship).
9. *Shakubuku Kyōten*, p. 406.
10. Kasahara, Kazuo, *Kakumei no Shūkyō* (The Revolutionary Religion) (Jinbutsu Ōraisha, Tokyo, 1964), pp. 298–299.
11. *The Nichiren Shoshu Sokagakkai* (The Seikyō Press, Tokyo, 1966), p. 182.

6. Religion and Politics

1. *Nichiren Shō-shū Sōka Gakkai* (The Sōka Gakkai of the Nichiren Shō Denomination) (Tokyo University *Lotus Sūtra* Study Society, Aoki, Tokyo, 1962), pp. 480–481.
2. This was the subject of an article by Yoshirō Tamura in *Daihōrin* (September, 1962).
3. Ramseyer, Robert, "The Sōka Gakkai and the Japanese Local Elections of 1963," *Contemporary Religions in Japan*, IV.4 (December, 1963), pp. 287 ff.

7. Theory, Doctrine, and Faith

1. *Kachiron* (Theory of Value), Tsunesaburō Makiguchi, Sōka Gakkai (1956), fourth edition, by Jōsei Toda, editor, 255 pp.
2. Translation of a poem by Taira no Kanemori in the *Hyakunin Isshu* collection of poems.
3. Makiguchi, *Kachiron*, pp. 166 ff.
4. *Ibid.*, pp. 167 ff.
5. *Ibid.*, p. 166.
6. The atitude presented in the book produced by the Tokyo University *Lotus Sūtra* Study Society is much more conciliatory than the traditional one represented by Kodaira in *Sōka Gakkai*, written four years earlier (in 1958).
7. See Ikeda, Daisaku, *Science and Religion* (The Sokagakkai Press, 1965), pp. 24–26, for an explanation of the "three proofs."

8. A Pilgrimage to the Foot of Mt. Fuji

1. Lloyd, *op. cit.*, p. 295, a footnote.
2. Basham, A. L., *The Wonder That Was India* (Sidgwick & Jackson, London, 1956), p. 127; revised edition (Hawthorn Books, Inc., New York, 1963), p. 128.

A SELECTED BIBLIOGRAPHY
OF WORKS IN ENGLISH

General

Anesaki, Masaharu, *The Religious Life of the Japanese People*, K. B. S., Tokyo, 1938.

———, *History of Japanese Religion*, London, 1930.

Armstrong, R. C., *An Introduction to Japanese Buddhist Sects*, private printing by Hunter Tose Co., Ltd., Canada, 1950.

Basham, A. L., *The Wonder That Was India*, Sidgwick & Jackson, London, 1956 (reprint); Hawthorn Books, Inc., 1963 (revised).

Callaway, T. N., *Japanese Buddhism and Christianity*, Shinkyo Publishing House, Tokyo, 1957.

Conze, Edward, *et al.*, *Buddhist Texts Through the Ages*, Philosophical Library, Inc., New York, 1954; Torchbooks, Harper & Row, 1959.

de Bary, William T., Jr., *et al.*, eds., *Sources of the Japanese Tradition*, Columbia University Press, New York, 1958.

Elliot, Sir Charles, *Japanese Buddhism*, Edward Arnold and Co., London, 1935.

Humphreys, Christmas, *Buddhism*, Penguin Books, Ltd., London, 1954 (reprint); Barnes & Noble, New York, 1962.

Living Buddhism in Japan, Bulletin No. 6, Part 2, International Institute for the Study of Religions, Tokyo, May, 1959.

Masutani, Fumio, *A Comparative Study of Buddhism and Christianity*, The Young East Association, Tokyo, 1957.

Murdoch, James, *A History of Japan*, Kobe, London, 1903–26; Frederick Ungar Publishing Company, New York.

Radhakrishnan, Sarvepalli, and Moore, C. A., eds., *A Source Book in Indian Philosophy*, Princeton University Press, 1957.

Reischauer, A. K., *Studies in Japanese Buddhism*, The Macmillan Company, New York, 1917.

Religion and Modern Life, Bulletin of the International Institute for the Study of Religions, Tokyo, November, 1958.

Sansom, George B., *Japan: A Short Cultural History*, Appleton-Century-Crofts, Inc., New York, 1940 (revised 1962).

Suzuki, Beatrice Lane, *Mahayana Buddhism*, Ruskin House, London, 1959.

The "New Religions" and New Movements in Old Religions

Contemporary Religions in Japan, quarterly journals published by the International Institute for the Study of Religions, Tokyo, from Vol. I, No. 2, June, 1960, to the present.

Hammer, Raymond, *Japan's Religious Ferment*, SCM Press Ltd., London, 1961; Oxford University Press, New York, 1962.

Japanese Religions, quarterlies issued by The Christian Center for the Study of Japanese Religions, Kyoto, from 1959.

McFarland, H. Neill, *The Rush Hour of the Gods*, The Macmillan Company, New York, 1967.

Offner, C. B., and Van Straelen, H., *Modern Japanese Religions*, Rupert Enderle, Tokyo, 1963; Twayne Publishers, Inc., New York, 1963.

Schiffer, Wilhelm, "New Religions in Postwar Japan," *Monumenta Nipponica*, XI, 1, 1955.

Schneider, D. B., *Konkōkyō, a Japanese Religion*, I. S. R. Press (International Institute for the Study of Religions), Tokyo, 1962.

Thomsen, Harry, *The New Religions of Japan*, Charles E. Tuttle Co., Tokyo, 1963.

Watanabe, Baiyū, "Modern Japanese Religions, Their Success Explained," *Monumenta Nipponica*, 1957, XIII, 1–2.

Nichiren Buddhism

Anesaki, Masaharu, *Nichiren the Buddhist Prophet*, Harvard University Press, Cambridge, 1916.

Kern, H. (translator), *The Saddharma-Pundarīka, or the Lotus of the True Law*, Sacred Books of the East, F. Max Müller, ed., Clarendon Press, Oxford, 1909. (Translated in 1884.)

Lloyd, Arthur, *The Creed of Half Japan—Historical Sketches of Japanese Buddhism*, John Murray, London, 1911.

Murano, Senchu, "The Eventful Life of Nichiren," *Young East*, Vol. 3, July, 1952.

Nichiren, *Kanjinshō*, translated by Senchu Murano, The Young East Association, Tokyo, 1954.

Richard, Timothy, *The New Testament of Higher Buddhism*, T. & T. Clark, Edinburgh, 1910.

Soothill, W. E., *The Lotus of the Wonderful Law or the Lotus Gospel*, Clarendon Press, Oxford, 1930.

Woodard, W. P., "The Wartime Persecution of Nichiren Buddhism," TASJ, Tokyo, 1959, Third Series, Vol. VII.

Sōka Gakkai

Contemporary Religions in Japan, published by the International Institute for the Study of Religions, Tokyo, I.1 (1960), II.1 (1961),

II.2 (1961), III.3 (1962), IV.4 (1963), V.2 (1964), and V.3 (1964).

Ikeda, Daisaku, *Change of Character (Ningen kakumei)*, a serial in *The World Tribune*, Los Angeles, 1965.

————, *The Human Revolution*, Vols. I, II, III, The Seikyō Press, Tokyo, 1966–67.

————, *Lectures on Buddhism*, Vols. I and II, The Seikyō Press, Tokyo, 1962.

————, *Science and Religion*, The Sokagakkai Press, 1965.

Makiguchi, Tsunesaburō, *Philosophy of Value* (a translation of *Kachiron*, revised and edited by Jōsei Toda), The Seikyō Press, Tokyo, 1964.

The Nichiren Shoshu Sokagakkai, The Seikyō Press, Tokyo, 1966.

Sōkagakkai, The, The Seikyō Press, Tokyo, 1960.

"Sōka Gakkai, A Strange Buddhist Sect," Sakae Kobayashi, *The Japan Christian Quarterly*, XXIV.2, 1958.

Toda, Jōsei, *Essays on Buddhism*, The Seikyō Press, Tokyo, 1961.